Condoms  are Cheaper

Than Child Support

&

Other Obvious Truths We Overlook

When Creating our Reality

To Grady
Thank you for the
with Love
Support

Christy Gaynell

Thompson Publishing

Condoms Are Cheaper Than Child Support

Written by Christy Gaynell

Illustrated by Javyn M Booth

Edited By Stacey-Jocelyne Lewis

Published by Thompson Publishing
ISBN 978-0-9882075-0-9

First Paperback edition

Dedication

This book is dedicated to everyone who contributed to the writing of it, either knowingly or unknowingly. Thank you for sharing your experiences with me, and giving me permission to share them with the world in the hope that someone may benefit from them.

I humbly extend a special thanks to my children and my parents who permitted me to publish the truth as I saw it, even at the risk of potential embarrassment. I thank you, and I love you very much.

~

I would also like to designate a special dedication to the readers, without whom this book would be unnecessary. May you find at least one insight that will forever change your life or at least your perspective of life.

Christy Gaynell

Table Of Contents

Part 3

Obvious Truths About Parenting

Part 4

Obvious Truths About Work

Part 1

Obvious Truths About Life

"Life is an opportunity, benefit from it.
Life is beauty, admire it.
Life is a dream, realize it.
Life is a challenge, meet it.
Life is a duty, complete it.
Life is a game, play it.
Life is a promise, fulfill it.
Life is sorrow, overcome it.
Life is a song, sing it.
Life is a struggle, accept it.
Life is a tragedy, confront it.
Life is an adventure, dare it.
Life is luck, make it.
Life is too precious, do not destroy it.
Life is life, fight for it."
— Mother Teresa

Healing Happens At The Hurt

As an alternate title for this chapter I considered using *"You can't heal your heart by massaging your vagina."* I still think that it may have been more appropriate. I find that with external injuries like cuts, and sprains, we go to the source to treat the injury with pain cream and a bandage, protecting and supporting the wound while it heals. However, for some reason, we do not follow the same logic when it comes to internal injuries like a hurting heart, a fractured mind, or a broken spirit.

We invest our hearts in relationships where they end up getting mistreated, or broken, and then we try to heal them by getting drunk or high and having sex at random. The problem with this particular solution is that it serves only to compound the problem. Instead of healing our heart, we end up scarring our soul. Sure, for the moment it feels better because we have numbed the pain and diverted our attention away from its source. But the only way to truly heal is to focus our attention on the area that has been damaged.

When my children were little and they sustained injuries of a physical nature, they would bring their wound to me and display it with the request that I make them feel better. I would assess the extent of the damage and come up with an appropriate remedy to take the pain away. In some cases, all they required was a little attention, in which case I could simply kiss the affected area and instantly they would feel better.

Mind you, it never helped to kiss any area other than the affected area. I know because I tried. My child would come to me with a scratch on his knee and say, "Mommy, kiss it." I would kiss his elbow. "That's not where it hurts," he would say to me. "Mommy you have to kiss my knee." I would then kiss his finger but still he would not feel better. We could play this game for as long as it took me to kiss the injury, and the moment I did, he was convinced that the pain had subsided.

For deeper cuts, scrapes, or wounds, other things were required. Band-Aids were needed if there was blood, Neosporin for pain, alcohol or hydrogen peroxide to stave off infection. For a major sprain or broken foot, an air boot, or cast, and crutches were necessary to support the injury while it healed. In each case, it had to be applied directly to the wound because that is where the pain originates and where the healing takes place.

Unfortunately, in the medication age, we are not taught

that our bodies heal themselves; that the drugs and medications doctors prescribe for us are only useful in masking the symptoms while our bodies do the work. We are not taught to wait patiently for the healing process to complete itself or what to do to increase the speed of recovery. We are especially not taught how to heal emotional wounds.

So when my son got older, and his hurts were of an emotional nature and no longer a physical one, he did not know how to show me the wound and ask me to heal it. In fact, he did not even believe I could. He found himself so overwhelmed with emotional pain that he decided to alleviate it himself by replacing it with physical pain.

When he was in middle school and the girl he liked, or rather the girl he had prayed for, broke up with him, he was so overwrought that he started cutting himself. He very gently and repeatedly slid a butter knife over his arm until his brain recognized that there was a more pressing issue to deal with than his breakup and redirected its focus.

In his case, he stopped short of drawing blood, which indicated to me that his fear of doing himself more harm was greater then the emotional pain he was feeling. Additionally, the fact that he let me see his wound "accidentally" was indicative of his awareness that causing physical pain was only a temporary fix. He inherently knew he needed a lasting solution, and subconsciously, he hoped that I would see his pain and make it better.

I am so grateful that I was able to recognize what was going on and help him work through his heartbreak by means of compassionate conversations and understanding. I wish that I could offer similar assistance to all of the people suffering. I know there are so many children and young adults out there who have loving parents with busy schedules, and little awareness of what signs to look for; that is assuming the person in question displays any signs at all.

Pain, whether it is physical or emotional, is your body's way of telling you something is wrong. It is like an alarm clock, waking you up to what is going on inside of you. The more you ignore your body's natural alarm, the more insistent it will get. If you want to quiet the pain and make it go away permanently, you have to feel it. You have to acknowledge the pain and its purpose while resolving to not add to the injury. In many cases, this alone is enough to make the pain go away. However, there are times when a little more effort is required, as I will discuss later.

They say time heals **all** wounds, but the truth is time only heals the wounds that are properly set and supported. No amount of time will heal a broken limb if you don't first push it back in place and then tightly bandage or cast it. With emotional pain, the same is true, and sometimes, the waiting process feels unbearable.

Many people find emotional pain more intolerable than physical pain and would do just about anything to keep from experiencing it fully. So instead of waiting it out or actively working to heal it, we increase the number of injuries we have. Like my son, we supply our brain with any means of diversion we can think of. In his case, it was physical pain. In other cases we may divert our pain with sex, overeating, drinking alcohol, or using drugs, which impair the body.

Overeating and drinking alcohol affect the body through weight gain and decreases in organ functionality, though they do tend to temporarily calm the mind. As long as you are using them, drugs create the illusion that everything is fine, but when they start wearing off, the sensation of pain is so greatly magnified, you feel compelled to immediately return to the bliss of being high. Certain substances have been known to fracture the mind, in some cases permanently, and they can be very addictive.

Sex is different in that it affects the soul. A lot of people think sex is a purely physical act. When they can't see any physical manifestation of the harm that comes from sex they think they are not causing any harm. This could not be farther from the truth. In fact, the harm you do is far greater because sex is not just a physical act, but also a spiritual one. And every time you have sex that is not in line with your spirit, you cause a little damage to your spirit and create a small scar on your soul.

You cannot see this occur anymore than you can see the existence of your spirit or your soul. However, it is reflected in your eyes if you look deep enough, in your behavior, and in your rapidly shifting perceptions on life, love, and happiness.

A broken spirit causes everything in life to hold less and less meaning until nothing seems to have any meaning at all. Sex becomes just an act to take the edge off, a means of scratching an itch, or getting a fix. It is no longer the bonding experience it was designed to be. The connection becomes blocked, and it fails to serve the purpose of uniting two spiritual beings together to form one soul.

All of these acts slow down the healing process. They pull the healing energy away from the original wound in order to repair all of the new injuries being created by this destructive behavior. If this goes on too long, the end result is at least one open wound that never heals properly. Over time, you forget the original source, or cause of the pain, making it much harder to completely heal.

We become so damaged that we begin to no longer even see healing as an option. We succumb to our addictions in whatever form they take until they no longer do the trick. Then, we search for something stronger until there's nothing more to find. We do all of this because no one told us that the key to our recovery is in our very own mind. The solution to every problem, the secret to healing every hurt, lives inside of our mind and beats inside of our heart.

Sadly, when it's the heart that needs the healing, we want the beating to stop. We don't even care if that means the breathing will stop.

It is imperative in healing the heart to focus our attention on the sources of our emotional pain, and treat our aching heart with the same level of care and attention we would give to broken bones or torn ligaments. We must guard our heart and shift it out of harm's way; protect and nurture it taking care to massage, pamper, and fill it with the love it feels it is missing; then our heart can heal properly without the hole, and without the loss of our precious soul.

These words are not intended as medical advice or as a substitute for a physician's instructions. However, my favorite methods for treating emotional pain are crying, laughing, and Inner Smile Meditation.

According to The Meditation Bible, Inner Smile Meditation promotes awareness of your internal body and organs, prevents illness, and promotes healing. The practice basically encourages you to smile into every gland and organ in your body, including the heart, and offer thanks for the work it does or use your smile to soften any tension found internally.

Talking to your body also helps to reduce pain release stress and assist in the healing process. Asking the aching or inflamed areas what is wrong or what it wants is extremely beneficial. If you listen closely, it will tell you exactly what you need for optimal health. Acknowledge the cause of any blocks or problems, and declare your intentions to make it right.

Often, this helps relieve pain almost immediately. For God fearing people, prayer works wonders as well.

I think the most important thing to remember is the heart is an organ that is also a muscle, which can be pulled, torn, injured, or broken. When this happens, it requires time and patience to heal just like any other muscle. You need to baby it, not abuse it, and acknowledge it, not deny it. The more time and attention you give your heart, the healthier, and better equipped it will be to handle the next opportunity it is given to love.

Action Plan: For Healing the Heart, Spirit, and Mind

1. Laugh and cry out loud and with abandon as often as you can. Laugh until you cry and cry until you laugh. Not only is it a cathartic release, but it may also help in the prevention of cancer.
2. Go for walks in nature and observe its magnificence. Seeing the perfection in nature helps us to see the perfection in ourselves.
3. Read inspired writings. Sometimes, when we can't hear spirit or feel inspired, we can benefit from reading the work of someone who could.
4. Write a journal chronicling how you feel and why you feel that way. You will recognize the lasting benefits of

14

this when you go back years later and read what you wrote, only to realize it is a less enlightened version of your current perspective.

5. Talk. Put the pain into words, and push the words out of your mouth and into the ears of anyone who will listen without bias, or judgment. If you don't know such a person, then see a therapist or call a help hotline if you can't afford professional help. By all means, find a way to express what you feel. The more ways you can find to push the hurt out, the less internal damage it will cause.

6. Last but not least, do one meaningful thing for yourself every week. It could be a hot bath or a spa day, as long as in doing so, you are declaring to yourself that you are worthy.

2

No One Can Make You Happy If You're Not

Happiness for me was sitting on the front porch of a basement apartment in Bequia, St. Vincent & the Grenadines. The apartment overlooked the ocean, and the man with whom I was in love was sitting near enough to touch. In that instant, I felt this sensational joy, and I immediately recognized it. I smiled to myself knowingly, and in the very next moment, I judged it. How can I be so happy when my children aren't here with me?

I examined my happiness, after which I questioned my judgment until finally I accepted it. There was no getting around the truth; I was genuinely, indubitably happy. My heart was filled with joy, my mind was free of fear, and in that moment there was nowhere else I would have preferred to be.

Those periods of unequivocal bliss made it well worth the hell I went through to get there. The night before I was supposed to leave for my trip, I had a huge fight with my stepfather, who had only just learned of my plans to return to the islands and decided that he didn't want me to go. In an attempt to stop me, he told me I was not permitted to stay at the hotel he owned.

I felt hurt. I had just spent the entire season prior living in the hotel and working to help build up the business out of a desire to see my parents succeed with their health intact. Now, I was being forbidden to stay there.

It was distressing, but it was not the first time I had found myself on a flight to a foreign country with no idea where I would stay upon arrival. I had very little money and a great deal of faith, which I must say, served me very well.

When I arrived in St. Vincent, I asked a taxi driver if he knew of a reasonable place for rent by the night. Fortunately for me, he had an uncle with space available. He drove me to the house, and I was able to negotiate a price within my budget to rent for the night. I needed to regroup and figure out what I was going to do about housing for the rest of the month. That night I tossed and turned until all of the stress was released into the bed. I awoke hopeful and positive it would all work out for the best.

Still, it took a lot of deep breaths, and a few short prayers, to help me build up enough courage to call the person I was flying there to meet and tell him what was going on. He told me not to worry; he would work something out. Suddenly, I felt a wave of relief wash over me.

Soon after I hung up with him, my mother called to tell

me she had arranged a room for me, if I needed it. I was grateful for her assistance, but I was much more delighted by the fact that the man I was going to meet was taking care of it.

In all of my stress, worry, and fear, I missed the first ferry and ended up spend the day joyously exploring the island of St Vincent before catching the evening boat to Bequia.

I walked off the ship to see him standing there waiting for me, and I knew everything was going to be fine. What I could not have anticipated, though, was just how well he would care for me. Being in his presence and in his arms allowed me to release all of the stress and anxiety I had been toting on my shoulders like another piece of luggage. I didn't even care that the brother of another guy I was previously seeing had just spotted us walking down the street together. Of course I knew it was going to get back to the other guy, but that didn't matter to me; I was happy.

It was then that I redefined my beliefs about happiness. I came to see happiness as a drug that created a state of euphoria so exquisite and ineradicable that nothing else mattered. Previously, I believed happiness stemmed from the feeling that all of the struggle, discomfort, and fear are worth the effort. But that theory seemed to be lacking something fundamental because it conflicted with my belief that we should not have to struggle in order to be happy. I believed that we should be happy in spite of struggle, not because of it, and that is exactly what I was.

I was two weeks in with only a couple of weeks left to spend with him before I thought about the fact that I had absolutely no idea what I was going to do when I returned home to the states. I had no place to live, no job, no money, no car, and two kids to support. The responsible parent in me would like to say that I was concerned, but for that month all I could be was blissfully happy. At that time, and in that place, those precious moments were all that mattered. I was sure I would figure the rest out later, but I was determined to enjoy being happy for as long as I could make it last.

I have since contemplated what happiness really is and where it comes from. The apple dictionary defines it as "feeling or showing pleasure or contentment," but I have been content, and it did not feel the same as being happy. The difference between the two is like the difference between loving someone and being in love. The latter allows you to exist in a relaxed and pleasant state, while the former excites your senses; it wakes you up, and makes you feel alive. Knowing this, I began to ponder; do you have to be in love to be happy?

The answer is decidedly no, and yes. To be happy, you do not necessarily have to be in love with another person, though it most certainly helps. However, you do have to be in love with some aspect of life. You could be in love with your job, your hobby, or even the act of living. The best is when you are in love with yourself, for if you achieve this most difficult feat, you will always be happy.

When you are in love with something outside of yourself, the happiness is fleeting; it lasts only as long as the thing you are in love with is accessible to you. Lasting happiness only happens when you are in love with yourself. Because you are the only constant in your life, you can be assured that no matter what happens in your life, you will be there for it, and if you love yourself, it makes every experience of living that much greater; including being in love with other people.

There was a point during my liaison with the aforementioned person that the relationship appeared to be ending, and my heart felt like it was being crushed in a vice grip. It was then that I knew how a person could want to end his or her life over the loss of love. I had never understood it before, but this time I could feel the emotion that was connected to that impulse. Had I loved him more than myself, I might have joined the ranks of the people on the suicide watch list.

Fortunately, I was in love with life and myself. Both meant more to me than losing him. My love for this sensational life allowed me to embrace the excruciating pain in the pit of my stomach. I attempted to neither escape it, nor numb it. My desire to experience all that life has to offer made me want to feel this as fully and deeply as I had experienced and felt happiness, and when the pain finally lessened, I felt I was the better for it. I was actually happy to have had that experience.

What the experience taught me is that we cannot depend on another person to make us happy. True happiness comes from seeing in yourself the same value you seek in others and holding the highest level of admiration and regard for yourself.

When you approach life from that perspective, you will reflect that out onto the world and enhance every life you touch. You will be happy with whomever you meet because you won't settle for someone who stands in the way of your being who you inherently are. People will actually be clamoring to get to you in the hopes that some of what you have will rub off on them.

My advice, then, is to treat yourself like you are your first love. See yourself through rose-colored glasses, and observe all of the beauty that lies within. Regard every encounter, event, and interaction as if it were a gift being presented to you for your personal pleasure. Do not judge anything as good or bad; just receive it with gratitude for the opportunity to experience something so amazingly pleasant or, in some cases, so wonderfully painful.

When you can lift your head up while facing your greatest fear and smilingly say with all honesty, "I am happy," then you will know, as very few do, what true happiness feels like.

Action Plan: For Falling in Love with Yourself

1. Get to know you. Write down everything you know about yourself, what you like, love, and detest.
2. Ask your friends what they know about you. What lights you up from the inside out? What are your favorite topics of conversation? What are your favorite things to do?
3. Finally, court yourself. Treat yourself like a person you were in a new relationship with, and put your best foot forward. Give yourself more of the things you like, and less of the things you don't like.
4. Evaluate how you would like to be treated by the people in your life. Create a list of people who treat you as you desire and make another list for those who leave a lot to be desired.
5. Make an effort to show appreciation for the people who treat you well. Observe the areas in which you will need to retrain the people who do not currently treat you the way you would prefer.
6. Realize that you can only change another person by changing yourself. You therefore do not retrain people by trying to change them, but by defining what you will, and won't tolerate from them. When you create and respect your own boundaries, others will too.

3

Condoms Are Cheaper Than Child Support

One of the first thoughts that come to mind when reading this title is, "well that's obvious." This is fitting only because, while growing up, my family jokingly referred to me as a prophet of the obvious. They said I would often point out the most apparent things as if no one could see them but me.

I have grown, learned, and matured since then, but still I feel the need to point out life's most conspicuous truths. It's not that I don't believe anyone else can see what I see; it's that whether or not people see it, not enough is being done about it.

This particular matter regarding child support is one that is close to my heart and my purse. I turned it into a joke on stage for the same reason I am writing about it now. Although it is common sense, I feel like people—men especially—need to hear it.

For years I tried to make my ex-husband hear me when I said this but to no avail. He now has five children by four different women, and the child support pot is spread so thin that I can barely pay my bills with my portion, and I have two of his children.

Now I know some of you are thinking that the purpose of child support is not for the receiver of it to pay personal bills and expenses, but that it should be strictly relegated to the care of the children. Though I understand this perspective, I do not share it. I personally believe that whatever monies enter a household are dispersible at the householder's discretion and are therefore subject to use as said person sees fit. That however, is neither here nor there because the opinions regarding this bone of contention have no bearing on the matter at hand.

The issue is that many men, like my ex-husband, enjoy the feeling of being inside of a woman so much that they are willing to forego wearing a condom. Some of them rely on luck, prayer, and pulling out as methods of birth control. Let me say for the record that when the luck runs out, the prayer, and pulling out no longer work either. The pulling out method has an even more diminished rate of effectiveness if a man gets so caught up in the heat of the moment that he forgets or opts not to pull out.

So many men take a devil may care, "I will deal with the consequences later," approach to life that I feel inclined to help them understand and appreciate what the consequences truly are.

The possible consequence of ejaculating one time inside of one woman without protection is one or more children. For each child that is born, you as the father will be expected to pay approximately twenty percent of your income every month, for eighteen years, or until said child graduates from college.

Let's do the math. Say for example you earn twenty-four thousand a year; this equals two thousand dollars a month before taxes. That means you will be required to give four hundred dollars a month, every month, to the mother of your child after Uncle Sam takes his cut out of your check. Four hundred a month times twelve, is four thousand eight hundred dollars a year. Multiply that by eighteen years, and you have eighty six thousand four hundred dollars. Now mind you, that is the absolute **minimum** you will have to pay. This does not even take into account any money you will spend on the child while he or she is with you, or what you have to pay in medical insurance and miscellaneous expenses. These are just the bottom line numbers based on the assumption that there is no change in your financial situation over the course of that eighteen-year period.

Some women are probably looking at this equation as a lucrative business opportunity. Their logic being, "If I get five men to give me four hundred dollars a month for having their babies, I wont have to go out and get a real job." Men, do not be deceived! There **are** women out there who think like this. Usually, they are looking for opportunities with higher income potential, such as athletes or entertainers. That way they only have to have one or two children to sustain their desired lifestyle, but the principle is the same.

To these women, I just want to say, please do not be fooled. Raising a child is work. It is a full-time job at which you earn every single penny you receive in child support. If you're trying to get pregnant strictly for the money, you would be better off seeking income with benefits, vacation time, and set hours. If you are doing it because you believe you want a child, then do that child you want a favor. Give him or her the privilege of an opportunity to be raised by two people who truly want to be parents; not one person who wants to be a mother and a man who was mislead.

Now, back to the men. Putting how it feels aside for a minute, let's look at sex and reproduction from a purely logical and monetary perspective. A condom costs two dollars each, at the most, and can be picked up for free at most clinics. A baby costs nearly a hundred thousand dollars over the course of eighteen years, and then there's college. An abortion costs less than a child but more than a condom, and it comes at a heavy emotional price. Which is the better option?

I know I said that this information and the answer to the above question is an obvious one, but I will say it again, because it deserves repeating. **Condoms are cheaper than child support**, and if you don't heed my warning, or ladies, if you catch a man who knows better but still has no interest in protecting himself, you both deserve to reap what you sow.

As for the child you bring into the world, I wish him or her love and happiness. The other day I looked at my own son and reflected on his pedigree thinking, "I am going to have to ingrain this in his mind so indelibly, that whilst all of his other thoughts are following the blood flow from one head to the other, this one will remain." Perhaps that way, he won't make choices that lead to unnecessary consequences.

Action Plan: For Personal Protection

1. The best option is of course celibacy. If you can't be celibate until you are ready to be a parent, get some protection and use it.

2. Educate yourself on how best to use your preferred choice of protection. Be sure to choose the right type, size, and brand to avoid discomfort and irritation.

3. Make sure you are meeting the needs of both parties by the protection of choice.

The Golden Rule

Do unto others, as you would have them do unto you. How often do we ignore this advice, opting instead to treat people the way we perceive ourselves being treated by them? You are doing yourself a huge disservice by behaving this way, and I beseech you, if you love yourself even a little bit, stop.

Growing up, I was told I didn't have any feelings. I heard it so often I believed it. I operated on a daily basis from that perspective. I assumed that if I didn't have feelings other people didn't either; so surely my words were not going to impact or impede them in any way. I said whatever I wanted to whomever I chose with no regard for the bearing my words could have on another person's life. I knew I certainly didn't base my choices, thoughts, or feelings on what they said. I believed myself to be equally disregarded.

I was twenty-two the first time I realized people could be affected by my words. My best friend, who was pregnant at the time, had just gotten her hair done and asked me what I thought of it. Not knowing any better, I told her that she

28

looked like the dog from the Church's chicken commercial after Aunt Esther's wig fell on his head. I know it sounds insulting, but from my perspective, it was just an unfavorable truth, and she did not take it well. She went home and cried, and when I found out, I felt really bad. Now while I still believe that honesty is the best policy, I recognize now that it is okay to sprinkle it with sensitivity when delivering it. I did not know how to do that then.

After that incident, I accepted that women were sensitive, and that they had feelings, which could be hurt by my words, but I still did not believe the same was true of men. They seemed so aloof; I could not believe my words or actions could impact them in any way. I was wrong.

I eventually learned that people are affected and impacted by the same things regardless of gender. This was a revolutionary shift in my thought process. You see, before this change in my thinking, I was less likely to help a man assuming that he should be able to do for himself. I would give anything I could to assist a woman in need, especially a woman with children. However, I looked at men as though by helping them I would in some way bring harm to my children or myself.

The first step to changing my outlook was accepting the fact that both men and women have feelings. This also meant acknowledging that I had them as well. The next thing was coming to the understanding that by helping others, I was also helping myself.

This was more difficult for me to see. For at first when I assisted others, I looked for the reciprocation to come from them. When they did not respond in kind, I felt as though they had gotten the upper hand. I resolved to do unto others, as they had done unto me, that way I could ensure that no one got the better of me.

Ralph Waldo Emerson in his essay *Compensation* helped me to understand that if I was acting out of love, no one could ever take advantage of me. In my mind the reward attached to doing a favor, would be in the act itself, not in what I hoped to get out of it. When I began acting in harmony with this way of thinking, and stopped looking for the people whom I'd helped to return the favor, I noticed that everything I did came back to me. It did not come from the places I thought it ought to, but it most certainly came.

It was then that the admonition to "do unto others as you would have them do unto you" made sense. I had previously believed that following this rule had to do with the people. But this universal law is not about the people so much as it is about the act. What you put out comes back to you. If you put love out you get love back. If you put out hostility you get that back as well. Whatever you put into the universe when dealing with others is what returns to you when you don't see it coming.

I started reversing the cycles I was currently in and creating new more positive ones. I realized that my feelings were not being acknowledged because I did not acknowledge feelings. I became more sensitive and compassionate to other people.

I decided to start asking myself, "What would I want done for me if I were in that person's situation?" Then to the extent that I was able, I would do exactly that for the person looking to me for help.

After my thoughts changed, it was as if I resonated something different. People started coming to me randomly asking for all sorts of assistance, and to the extent that I could, I gave it. It was almost surreal how it would happen sometimes. If I was at a grocery store, strangers—often men— would come to me and ask me to buy them food, and I would. They always seemed so grateful, and I was happy to be in a position to do it. That I had enough of anything to give some away was a blessing in itself.

Then it got weird. One day a man came to the door of a house I was renting out, and asked me if he could sleep on the porch. I couldn't very well turn him away, but I was not the one living there. I consulted with the person who was living in the house, and she agreed to let the man sleep on the porch. She gave him a mat and a sheet to cover himself.

He stayed a few days, and then we had to make other arrangements because we were starting a daycare in the house, and we were concerned about how it would look to the mothers dropping their children off if a strange man was sleeping in front of the door.

I took the man to my other house on the other side of town and told him that if he needed a place to stay, he could stay there. He stayed for a while, took a nap, and then asked where he could go to catch a bus so that he could go to work. I drove him around searching for the nearest bus stop, but finding one was more trouble than I anticipated. I finally dropped him at a stop that was a considerable distance from the house, and he decided it would be inconvenient for him to stay there. I told him I would continue looking or see if some arrangements could be made to help him get to work easier, but he never came back. I rested easy knowing I had done everything I could to help. Still, I felt bad that the world had to be this way. With so many empty houses, there is no reason people should be living on the streets.

A couple of years later, I found myself in a similar situation. My house was in foreclosure and they were seeking to repossess my car, my money had all run out and I was left with nowhere to go. It was then that I saw the benefits of my actions. Between the kindness of strangers and loved ones I have not wanted for a single thing in the moments of my life that looked the bleakest. My children have remained well taken care of and scarcely aware of just how hard times have been for us.

Thus far, I have not gone a day without food, clothing, and shelter, and I believe it is because of the kindness I have shown to others in the past. My only wish now is that I had done more back then when I was in a position to do so. I regret that I lost sight of the universal laws and started holding on out of fear when I should have been letting go with faith. It is my hope that you learn from my experience, and come to understand as I have that you do unto yourself, as you do unto others.

Action Plan: For The Golden Rule

1. Treat everyone you encounter the way you would want to be treated if you were in his or her shoes
2. Expect nothing in return for your actions.
3. Act only out of love and remember Universal laws cannot be broken. Understand that for every action there is an equal and opposite reaction or consequence.

Figure Out Why You're Hungry Before You Eat

It was while fasting that I first came to understand the truth about food. It was my first time fasting, and I was doing the Master Cleanse, also known as the Lemonade Diet. I had read that it was supposed to help clean out your digestive tract and return your body to optimal health. As it was only supposed to last ten days, I thought that it should not be very difficult at all. I was wrong.

In the beginning, there were hunger pangs, and headaches coupled with low energy and irritation. I was not concerned because, from what I read, it was to be expected. Days three and four were relatively easy, but somewhere between days five and seven, something shifted. It was as if my body realized it wasn't going to get the food it was craving, and the cravings stopped.

What replaced them was the truth. For the first time, I was able to hear what my body really wanted and shocked to discover it wasn't food at all. On that occasion, I realized that what I was feeding with overly processed junk food was actually a craving for spirituality. I was hungry for wisdom, knowledge, and a connection to something greater than myself. I found some spiritual literature, and as I read it, my desire for Doritos and doughnuts went away.

On other days and at various times of day, I was made aware of other cravings that I had been improperly feeding. I was unknowingly starving for physical affection. I wanted to feel the touch of another person; preferably one that I had not given birth to. I typically fed this craving with French fries, and ice cream. I had cravings for sex that I fed with chocolate. The list went on and on, and let me tell you the process was painful. I was an emotional wreck because I was suddenly aware of all that was missing from my life.

By day eight, I had worked through the entire emotional trauma. I could no longer satiate myself with food, but I was hit with a consuming desire to chew. The cravings were gone and the hunger was at bay, but my oral fixation was rearing its ugly head, and my jaws were dying to chomp down on something. I was able to complete my ten days without giving in, but it was challenging.

When I returned to my typical diet, the food no longer tasted the same. It was actually quite disgusting. With every bite I thought, "What on earth would make a person eat this crap?" I put the Pringles down, and waited a few minutes before taking a bite of the chocolate chip cookie. None of it tasted good anymore, but I resolved to push through, and keep eating until I was once again properly addicted. Then the taste didn't matter because the craving for it was stronger than the flavor.

What I walked away with though, what stuck with me, even after I went back to eating devitalized food, is that there is a problem with the way we conceptualize food in this country. Obesity is at epidemic proportions, and we want to blame the overweight people for not having self-control. The problem is not a lack of self-control. If you think about it, the only thing keeping the majority of "normal" people at their desired size is medication, be it for anxiety, weight loss, or stress.

Pharmaceuticals are a trillion dollar industry, and the preponderance of diet pills on the market is a clear indication to me that keeping people overweight is part of the plan. How else will companies get consumers to buy weight loss drugs? If you're questioning my logic here, think about the fact that food and drugs are governed and regulated by the same agency. The FDA has jurisdiction over what is permitted to go into both the food and the anti-food.

What is most disturbing is how deeply we buy into it. My own brother can consume with me what I call a meal, and upon completion of it he will say, "Okay, now I'm hungry. Let's go get some food."

To which I will respond, "We just ate." Because the way I see it, the fruit we had just eaten was the best meal for us.

"No," he says, "I mean some real food."

So I inquire about what he regards to be real food, to which he replies, "Let's go get some McDonald's, or Waffle House, or something, you know something with some meat, some sausage, or pancakes, eggs, grits, all that."

We had a similar conversation at dinner when he told me that vegetables are not real food and that he was allergic to them. According to him, cheeseburgers and hot dogs are real food. Steak and potatoes are a meal for a man, and lobster and shrimp are high-class food. After having conversations like this, I had to wonder, what is wrong with our minds?

How can we believe that the food man created is better for us than the food that God created? How can we reconcile in our mind that the junk food laden with additives, addictive substances, and preservatives is somehow better than what grows on a tree created just for us? For those that believe in the Bible, there is a scripture that reads, "Just as he feeds the birds so will we be fed," but we worry if we cannot afford to buy birds to feed to ourselves.

It just does not make sense that one could choose a lard-filled cookie as a snack over an apple and feel good about it because the package it came in says low fat. How do you tell yourself, "I am allergic to vegetables; they are not good for me; give me a hamburger instead?" What kind of logic is this that plagues our nation?

What's worse is that we know the effect it has on our

bodies. We know that it clogs our arteries, causes heart problems, makes us gain weight and feel lethargic. Some more informed people are even aware of its effects on our mental state. They know that certain foods lead to depression and lunacy, and still we eat them hand over fist as if no greater substance were ever created. Ironically, drugs like marijuana, which grows naturally, are mostly illegal as if potato chips and soda are not drugs.

Yes, our government greatly contributes to the problem. Processed food is a multibillion-dollar market. What do you expect? Of course the media is going to support them. Who do you think is supporting the media? Fast food companies are among the top spenders in media advertising. Many people argue that fast food is convenient, but is it really more convenient to sit in a drive-thru, and wait on someone to serve you, than it is to go in a store and buy an orange or banana, peel it, and eat it?

It's sad really; the vicious cycle in which food can keep you. I mean, it starts off innocently enough—you eat something not necessarily good for you because of peer pressure, or sense memory, or a craving, whatever the case may be.

For that moment, you feel great wondering how you ever thought you could give that food up. Then the chemical compound breaks down in your system and your initial euphoria begins to fall, and it brings you down right along with it. Suddenly, you are extremely sleepy, and you can't figure out why. Not only that, but your mood, which was so pleasant only a moment ago, is just barely tolerable—even to you now.

"What happened?" You wonder. If you are insightful, you realize that it is the side effect of the high carbohydrate or high sugar food you just ate. Now you feel guilty because you knew you should not have eaten it in the first place. So you go in the refrigerator and the cupboard looking for something comforting to eat to assuage your guilt, and the cycle is born. Comfort food can only lead to a greater need for comfort. This is why emotional eating is not healthy.

Please do not take anything I have said thus far personally, and do not be offended. Even though I keep saying you, I am speaking just as much of myself. We are all guilty of it and for the most part cannot help that we are that way, for we are conditioned to be so from infancy.

Yes, even before you could feed yourself, there were people around you trying to use food as a means to bring you comfort or at the very least shut you up. Nobody likes the sound of a crying baby; many people upon, hearing a baby cry, react by shoving a bottle in its mouth. It is a commonly accepted way of saying I don't know what's wrong with you, but I am certain food can fix it.

This often helps, not because the child is necessarily hungry, but because we are following the statute that was set in motion by the hospital staff at the medical center. You see, they have two goals regarding each baby that is born into their facility. The first goal is to get them out of the hospital as fast as they can without liability, and the second is to ensure that they come back regularly for as many reasons as possible. They accomplish that goal initially by making sure that babies were well on their way to a sugar addiction before they ever leave the hospital.

For a period of several decades, the hospital administration would give babies water that contained 5% sugar in the form of glucose. It was clearly labeled 5% glucose water and was strongly encouraged that parents gave this to their child. In most cases, the nurses would give the babies the glucose water before the child was ever even given to it's parents, and when people left the hospital they were given a couple of boxes to further increase the potential for addiction.

Doctors are well aware of all of the possible medical conditions that can stem from an addiction to sugar, so if they give you one before you leave them they know you will be coming back regularly. The same is true of many drug addictions. Most prescription drug addictions start in the hospital. That, however, is not the topic at hand.

As I mentioned before, the hospitals' primary goal is to get you out as quickly as possible. To be relieved of liability, they have to make sure that all of the patients' systems and organs are working properly. In order to do this, they have to feed newborns that may or may not be hungry to ensure that their digestive tracts are working.

They know full well that when babies are born they have enough nutrients and food in their system to sustain them for a few days, but instead of allowing a newborn to progress naturally to a state of hunger, they insist that the mother feed the child on their time frame, and if she is unwilling or unable for whatever reason, they feed the baby the crap they concocted in some laboratory and labeled food.

What the hell is in baby formula anyway, and what idiot convinced an entire nation that it was just as good for our babies as breast milk? Even a person subsisting on a diet of purely fast food can pass onto her newborn healthier milk than they will get from those processed store brands.

Making sure the digestive tract is functioning properly is crucial, but by not allowing the baby and mother to go through the natural process on their own time, there is no telling what forms of failure they may be setting us up for.

Some might argue that we have all been through it and grown up under the same process, and there is nothing wrong with us. I, however, am not satisfied that this is the whole truth. Is there really nothing wrong with us, or is that just what is most comfortable for us to believe? We live in a society full of people who do things indicative of a person who is mentally warped, and the vast majority of us live with an unnatural complacency, perfectly content to believe that there is nothing wrong with us.

Sometimes I just want to shout, "Wake up people! Think, feel, do something, anything to let us know you're alive!" It's like we thrive on contentment, and we are perfectly numb to any semblance of feeling lurking beneath our surface. Granted, that is not true of all of us; that is only true of those who use the wonderful drug we call food to numb the pain. The rest of us need something stronger and more stigmatic like drugs, and alcohol.

The bottom line is this. There are many systems of control set up to run this country and keep its citizens in a state of passive aggressive complacency, and to whatever degree possible, ignorance. Processed food and its mass distribution and commercialization are one of those systems. Now you can choose to continue eating the way you always have, or you can choose to do something different and be amazed at what you discover.

My challenge to anyone willing to take it is to start by doing thirty days of eating nothing but raw fruits and vegetables. If you take this challenge, please by all means contact me and make me aware of the effect this has on your life. If you are unable to make it the full thirty days, go for as long as you can, and at whatever point you feel compelled to give in to the pull of processed food, I want you to recognize your initial response to what you first eat.

What does the first bite taste like? What about the

second? How many bites does it take before it is good again? Change does not happen over night, but if you pay attention to what is going on internally, the desire to do something different will eventually begin to outweigh the desire to feed the addiction.

Action Plan: For Feeding the Hunger

1. Think before you snack. The next time you go to reach for food, ask yourself the following questions:
2. Am I really hungry?
3. What emotions am I feeding with this food?
4. Would I still want this if I felt satisfied with my life?
5. Is this food the best thing for me?
6. How will I be affected by this food 30 minutes from now?

6

You Have Power, Use It

When I was a little girl, I believed that I was a super hero. I thought it was my job to protect all of the little girls around me. I would spin around in circles and jump off of the largest rock on the playground and yell, "It's Christy time!" I would then chase all of the boys that were trying to harm the little girls in an effort to protect them.

I was six years old at the time, and I am not sure why at six I felt like little girls needed protecting, but I did, and I felt like it was my job to do so. On some level, it seemed to work too. I was never much for fighting, but I believed I was powerful and fear inspiring, and when I said, "It's Christy Time!" the boys would scatter like flies. They would run from me as if I were actually going to harm them.

Looking back, I suppose that it is probably just the nature of people, especially children, to run when being chased, but for me, at that time in my life, it was simply the most fun I could have at recess. I don't know why I adopted her, but it was nice to have an alter ego. She empowered me to

44

be who I was not. She was not shy or fearful at all. She believed that nobody could bring her harm, and as long as she was around, nobody was going to harm any other child either.

I wonder now what happened to me that made me see the world as being so bleak. Is that the normal thought process of a child? I know most children, predominantly boys, long to be like whatever super hero happens to be popular at the time, but I decided to embody my own personal super hero and protect people who could not protect themselves. I have felt compelled to do that my entire life, and I am curious to know if perhaps it is because I was unprotected.

Maybe at six years of age I needed a super hero, so I became what I was missing. What was so wrong in my life back then? Was it simply my parents' divorce, the home for battered women, living in our car, and my parents fighting to the point where my mom was breaking windows with her hands, and causing herself severe bleeding and scarring, or was there more?

Did there have to be more than that, or was that enough? At four years old, I felt like the protector of my mother and my brothers. I always felt compelled to help, heal, and care for people—not all people—but those that sincerely needed me. It seems strange now to think that a child would believe people needed her. Is that trait a characteristic of most children? Perhaps it is, and they just don't verbalize it. I didn't.

As I grew older I stopped calling myself "Christy Time,"

but I never did stop doing what I could to protect those that I felt needed me. For years it was my brother, the middle child, who I was always trying to protect. He seemed to need it so much. It was as if he did not feel he had a space of his own; he would go and invade other people's space. When he angered them to the point at which they wanted to cause him physical harm, he would retreat and come find me. I would then ward off any who would try to harm him.

Sometimes it was my other brother, and sometimes it was our father, but I didn't care who it was; I was not going to let anyone mistreat my brother or any other child in my presence for that matter.

In high school, I encountered girls who had suffered from various forms of sexual abuse, and I befriended them to give them a safe place to talk through all of the crap that comes with sexual abuse; the stuff they don't tell you about on TV.

TV is great for exposing how often and how many different ways a person can be sexually abused, but it does not tell you what happens when the abuse is over. It doesn't tell you about the stain you wear on your skin for the rest of your life that tells the world you are a victim of unspeakable acts. It doesn't tell you that your mindset and behaviors change–that your fear either increases, or goes away completely. No one tells you that you will be judged for actions of which you are not even aware, and that you only act that way as a result of a negative incident wherein you were stripped completely of control.

Television does tell you about the guilt you are liable to feel, but you don't really get an accurate understanding of why you feel guilty; you only know that you do. However, it doesn't tell you that because you have now been victimized, you are more likely to live that experience over and over again. Another thing it doesn't tell you is that certain people will target you because they recognize something lacking in you, and they desire to take advantage of it.

You may be targeted because you have lost your sense of boundaries, or your ability to say no, or even the feeling that you have the right to say no. It may be that predators see a longing in you for the protection you were lacking at the time or a stronger desire to be loved to offset the internal feeling of inadequacy. Whatever it is you feel, perpetrators can see it, and they will re-victimize you given a chance, especially if you don't work through the related issues.

The first step in working through a problem is acknowledging that it exists and talking about it. That is what I was there for. I was a great listener; understanding and empathetic, I would listen without judgment.

I noticed that a lot of people who had been through various trials and difficulties in life came out of them with amazing gifts. Some people could not remember the experience but were able to use the gift to prevent or deter reoccurrences, and other people could not tap into their gift until they had dealt with the problem.

These gifts take many forms but they are all pretty amazing. Some people have the ability to see an aura around every person they meet. When people are presented to them, a colored light appears around them, which gives these people tremendous insight as to what type of person they are dealing with.

Other people just get a sense that something isn't right with certain people, and they know to stay away. Some are given the gift to listen and draw people out of their shell or into conversation, and others have the ability to heal, but for this to work there must be tremendous faith on both sides.

There are those who can see in the dark, and there are others who can't see at all but can hear danger in the sound of a voice. Some of us have what at times can appear to be super human strength, and for others their weakness is their protection. Some people believe they have super powers, and other people think that these abilities are just a myth.

The truth lies somewhere in the middle. There are gifts and abilities given to all of us, but how powerful they are is determined by the extent to which we use them. Heightened intuition, or telepathy, is no different from having an amazing singing voice, or speed, or the ability to jump really high with a ball in your hand. The more you practice, the better you get at it. It's just sad that the talents of some are revered, while others are shunned and feared.

Really, what good is it to anyone if you have a gift and do not use it? Who benefits if you can sense that a person is in danger but do not warn them, or if you can feel where a person's pain is coming from but do not tell them what can take it away? What good are you to anyone if you can heal him or her with your touch and avoid him or her at all cost because of the depletion of energy it will create in you?

Yes, I acknowledge that tapping into your energy for the benefit of others is extremely draining, but there are ways you can replenish it. Sometimes, just seeing the effect of your actions is enough to restore most of what it took from you. Another option is doing something special for you; it may seem a little selfish but revitalization is necessary. Restoration can also come from another with a similar gift. It is important in dealing with these types to try to make the exchange reciprocal, so no one is left feeling drained, or depleted.

Clearly there are other people who also truly believe in super powers. Otherwise, they would not be portrayed in so many movies. Of course, in the movies, they are enhanced and exaggerated, but art does imitate life, doesn't it? What could be a more feasible outlet for exposing one's belief in people's ability to do things we see as uncommon, unnatural, or impossible than a fiction movie? When I watch movies like X-Men, The Matrix, or a television show called Heroes, I think to myself, there are others that know.

When my son was born, my first child, I noticed that he

was very sensitive, and had a deep love for people. I didn't much mind because I did not expose him to a lot of people, so I thought it was cute the way he developed an attachment to some of my friends, but I still didn't know how I would cope with his sensitivity. I sometimes had a biting tongue that would just rip him apart. He has helped me learn to control it; I should probably thank him for that.

Anyway, when he was around three years old, I realized that he was very intuitive, especially towards people he felt a connection to. He demonstrated this one day with a close friend of mine. He kept telling me to call her and see if she was okay; he said he thought something was wrong with her. He repeated it several times, as I was not paying him as much attention as I should have.

I did not call her. A couple of hours later, she called, and told me she had left work early because the bank where she worked had just been robbed. Furthermore, it was her teller window that the robber targeted. I asked her what time it happened, and surprisingly she said it was right about the same time my child was telling me to call her. I looked at him and thought, how could he know?

When he was six he came to me shyly and said, "Mom I have super powers."

"I believe you," I said, "So do I."

He thought I was joking with him so he said, "No, I'm serious Mom. I really do have super powers."

"I know you're serious, and I really believe you. What are your super powers?" I asked him.

He did not want to tell me at first, but then he said, "I don't know how to explain it. I just see things."

I told him I could too. He looked at me completely unsure of what to believe and decided to just accept what I was saying whether it was true or not.

To strengthen his belief in his own ability, I told him about an opportunity I had recently had to use my gift. I have the ability to feel other people's pain. When it is very intense sometimes I turn away from it because it is more than I can bear. However, if there is a life in danger, I will not turn away. I learned this one day last year when my best friend was talking to me on the phone and hung up rather abruptly because something was wrong with her daughter.

I went on with what I was doing when suddenly I had trouble breathing and a strange sensation in my stomach. I turned to my cousin, who was with me at the time, and I told her, "I can't breathe; only I don't think it's me. I think it is someone else. I think it is my friend's daughter."

I immediately started calling my friend back, and when I finally got her on the phone, I asked her if her daughter was having trouble breathing. She told me that she wasn't having trouble breathing but that she had broken out in a rash all over her skin. I told my friend to watch her carefully because I suspected that she would soon have a breathing problem as well. She asked what made me think that, and I told her about my experience. She agreed to watch her carefully, as I was not a person easily given to panic or unnecessary concern. In her opinion, my tendency was to under react if anything.

When I hung up, my breathing returned to normal, but the feeling in my gut was still there. I kept in constant communication with her throughout the rest of the day. Sometime that night, she called to tell me that her daughter was indeed having breathing problems. She asked me what she should do, and I told her simply to follow her strongest instincts. Anything she could be accused of overreacting by doing is what she should do.

Over the next day or two the symptoms came in waves with increasing intensity. The child had many allergies, but she could not figure out what could be causing an internal as well as an external reaction. She had little time to research all of the possibilities because she had to care for the child and try to make sure she did not get worse. I could feel what was going on, but I had no idea what I could do to change it.

Then I read something in a book called *The Alchemist* by Paulo Coelho. It said, "If you can feel something about some one else before it happens, then you are being given the opportunity to change it." So I prayed about it. I was growing very nervous because my gut was telling me there was a possibility the child was not going to survive this. I prayed very specifically and in great detail regarding this situation. I had to, as I had seen the possible outcome, and I knew it was something I was not at all comfortable with.

After I prayed, I called my friend's husband and told him he needed to go immediately home; his child's life depended on it. To this day, I am not sure if he hung up on me or we just got disconnected, but either way he went home. I then called my friend and told her what I had done. She told me he was on his way home, so I told her just don't let him leave. I didn't know how, or why, but her child's life depended on him staying home for the rest of the night.

"Ok," she said, "I will try." And she thanked me for my concern.

The next day she called me and told me that him staying home and sleeping with the child gave her time to do some research; what she found was a new chemical in her child's bubble bath that she was allergic to.

Apparently, when the child was bathing she drank some of the water and that caused the breathing problems while the direct contact with the soap had caused the bumps on her skin. That also explained why the bumps were under her clothes even though there was no change in laundry detergent. The reason the symptoms got worse the next day is because in an effort to calm her before putting her to bed on the first day of the outbreak, she gave her another bubble bath.

We both concluded that had her husband not been home, she probably would have given her another bubble bath to try and calm her down before bed instead of doing the research and home inspection that led her to uncover that the bubble bath was the culprit all along. Thank God we never have to know whether or not the child would have survived that.

After I relayed my story to my son, he felt satisfied that I was telling the truth and a little more connected to me, as if we belonged to a special club. I encouraged him to use his gifts wisely and never take them for granted. I worked to help him understand that his powers were precious, and that there were people in this world who would try to make him feel powerless; don't let them.

When it comes to your gifts and abilities, trust only your own inclinations. Disregard any who speak against what you know intrinsically to be true. I don't care if it is the media, the government, the religious leaders, your best friend, or your spouse. Trust yourself first.

Having said that, if you know that there are people who do not agree with what you know to be true, do not broadcast it. Don't bring attention to yourself with regard to your gifts unless it is necessary. If you must expose yourself, then do as the more successful people of the past have done and make it look like a work of fiction. Make it seem so unbelievable that people couldn't possibly think you were serious. Magic and theatre are excellent covers; just look at Criss Angel and his show *Mind Freak*. For that matter, look at this book. I couldn't possibly be serious, right?

I know many people will read this and assume, perhaps correctly, that I think too much of myself. However, I would rather think too much of myself, and use it to try to make a difference in the lives of others and myself, than not think enough of myself and do nothing at all. Earlier in the book I mentioned that I view what I once called super powers as gifts from God, and the experience I related above is one of the reasons.

Without prayer and God's help, none of the rest of it would have mattered. Without faith we may not have even prayed. Many people disregard the things they feel because they worry about how they will be perceived by onlookers. I believe that if they combine their gifts with heartfelt prayers, many miracles will occur. God did not give us talents only to watch us bury them; that, too, is written in the Bible.

Each and every one of us was given something. If you know what your gift, talent, power, or whatever else you may want to call it is, tap into it. Pray about it, and by all means use it. It's easy to get caught in the trap of letting how we think others will perceive us stop us from using our gifts. That is what those who would try to control you are counting on. Historically, the desire to control us by inspiring fear of these gifts was the purpose behind witch-hunts.

There are those that would say the experience I described above was just coincidence, and to them I say a positive coincidence in my opinion was better than the alternative. If even without my input everything would have been just fine, the possibility of an alternate ending was enough to make me speak up.

I know that there are others who have similar experiences because some have shared them with me. My own cousin for example is also capable of feeling and taking other people's pain. There have been times when we were together and one of us was in pain, and we could literally feel the pain transfer back and forth between us. We never felt it at the same time, but by verbal description we were feeling the same thing.

I hope that in writing this I will reach at least one person who silently believes in his or her ability to heal, cure, or change the outcome of events by whatever talent or gifts they have. I hope this will give that person enough courage, knowing they are not alone, to tap into it and make a difference. You never know whose life you may save or enhance.

Action Plan: For Using Your Super Powers

1. Recognize what your power is and acknowledge it.
2. Accept and appreciate your ability. Sometimes being gifted can feel like a curse, but it is important to learn to love and nurture it.
3. Practice, practice, practice; it is the only way to enhance, improve and perfect your gift.
4. Trust your inner voice knowing it's there for a reason.
5. Do not verbally express your talent unless the situation calls for it. Sometimes, telling people you have power makes them want to rob you of it.

Part 2

Obvious Truths About Relationships

"Some of the biggest challenges in relationships come from the fact that many people enter into a relationship in order to get something; they're trying to find someone who's going to make them feel good. In reality, the only way a relationship will last is if you see your relationship as a place that you go to give, and not a place that you go to take." -Anthony Robbins

You Attract What You Are, So Be Yourself

In each one of us, there exists the fear that if people really knew us they might not like us as much. We are afraid that were we to open up to people, we would be rejected, or outcast. In a nutshell, it is this fear of our own inadequacy that is responsible for our inability to be ourselves in the company of the people we most desire to accept us. This fallacious belief is given a heightened feeling of veracity when combined with the fear of loneliness.

Loneliness feels like desiring something you cannot have; or more specifically desiring someone, or the attention of a person, or people who are unwilling or unable to give you what you feel you need. Loneliness has little to do with being alone, for it is entirely possible to be completely alone and not feel lonely, just as it is possible to be surrounded by people and feel extremely lonely. More interesting is the fact that it's possible to be in the company of the person whose attention it is you want, and still feel lonely.

So what causes loneliness? It is caused by an inability to find people with whom we can relate. Imagine for a moment, there are seven billion people in the world, easily connected by travel, phone, or Internet, and so many of us have trouble finding even one single person we feel can relate to us. That is what loneliness feels like. So what do you do about it?

For the vast majority of us, the answer is nothing. We suffer in silence; hoping and praying for something to change. We wait, and we hope for a chance encounter with someone who can change our lives and bring us out of our increasingly depressing state. We exist behind a façade; a mask that we hope is hiding our internal pain from the judgmental masses. We go to places where other people will see us, and we smile, and laugh to appear that we are like them. We attempt to belong and behave as though we are no different than the people whose company we are in.

The reality is that, to a large degree, we are exactly who we pretend to be. For most of the people we end up surrounded by are also lonely and searching. They are in those places for the same reason and yearning for the same thing. We are all looking for companionship, understanding, love, and the ability to relate to another human being without having to pretend to be something or someone else. These are the most basic human needs and the most difficult for some of us to meet.

The cure for loneliness exists, and it is actually the cure

for many ailments. It can be summed up, quite simply, in two words: Be yourself. The more we try to hide who we are the less likely we will be to find someone who can relate to us because people can't see who we are.

If you only show the mask, then you will only attract people who relate to the mask. That is why so many of us continue to attract the wrong type of people and can't figure out why. We go out into the world and portray ourselves as other than what we feel we are and wonder why superficial or shallow people keep coming to us. We never stop to think that by wearing this mask on the surface, we attract people who don't see past the surface.

Take off your mask, be who you are, do what you love, and go to places where you actually enjoy participating in what is going on. Then you will no longer be lonely; not because the person you are looking for will magically show up, but because you are satisfying your own needs. Additionally, even though you may not find Mr. or Ms. Right, you may at least find a person with whom you can converse enjoyably on topics of mutual interest.

There was a time when I was willing to remain in a relationship with a guy I did not feel like I could communicate with just because I liked the way he made me feel when he put his arms around me. He brought me a level of comfort I didn't find in other people, and for that I loved him. It wasn't enough though; I kept wondering if at some point the lack of communication between us would bother me? Would I find myself years later trying to figure out how I ended up with a person with whom I couldn't share stimulating conversation?

I intuitively felt that he was extremely intelligent and knew quite a bit about a great many things. So I believed if we were to actually try and talk about, well anything, it probably would have been a very good conversation. In fact it happened once, and it was. It just wasn't consistent enough for me. At that point in my life, I was too impatient and self-sufficient to be satisfied with unrealized potential.

I often joke that my marriage taught me independence. Though I say it jokingly, the reality is that concerning my marriage, truer words were never spoken. It was not so much for lack of communication as it was for lack of physical presence.

After about the first year of my marriage, my husband no longer saw the importance of coming home at night. As a result, I spent many nights alone and learned to enjoy sleeping by myself. Then one day, he told me he was going out of town without me. I thought the only proper response to that was to tell him that when he returned I would be doing the same thing.

I refused to have a one sided relationship in which he felt he could just get up and go whenever and wherever he wanted while he left me at home alone with the kids. So when he told me he was going to Vegas with a bunch of guys from work and ended up in Jamaica with the girl he was sleeping with, he returned to find that I was going to Paris by myself.

It was the first time I had ever gone anywhere by myself, and this was not just anywhere. This was halfway around the world to a country where I barely spoke the language, and had no accommodations to speak of upon arrival. The ironic thing about this trip was that it was the first time in my life I found myself in a situation where I was completely alone, and one of the very few times I did not feel at all lonely.

I learned that sometimes loneliness or the fear of it is a way in which we allow others to control us. We allow ourselves to be deterred from doing, experiencing, and living because we don't have a person who will join us on the journey. We don't stop to think that if we just take the journey, we will meet the people along the way.

Since that trip I have been on a number of others, in and out of the country, with and without the company of others, and I can honestly say that some of the trips I took by myself are among my fondest memories and most enjoyable times. I discovered that being alone was a guarantee I would be in good company, but that is only because I like myself.

I cannot comment on what the experience would be like for a person who does not like him or herself, but for those of you who do, you know that your own company is sometimes the best company. Rarely is this truer than when traveling. I know there are a lot of people who will be very much against traveling alone and therefore upset with me for what appears like my advocation of it. So let me just say that while I do not advocate traveling alone for any who have fear regarding it I will say this: before making a decision for or against it, know your reasons.

The reason that so many people are against it is because of the well-publicized stories on the news, usually of women who have gone missing while on vacation in foreign countries. I do not let this deter me, as my reasoning on the issue is different. The way I see it, the people who go missing are usually not alone; they are either in pairs, or in groups, and when one girl disappears, we only know about it when the rest of the people come back and tell us about it, or they may both come up missing. Yet people come up missing in this country all of the time as well, so what really is the difference?

It doesn't matter where you come up missing if you're going to come up missing anyway. Whether it's Europe, Asia, Africa, or right here in America, the same fate can befall you at the same time in the same way; the only thing that changes is the location. But that's just my perspective. Feel free to make your own decisions. My only purpose and goal is to make you think.

So while you're thinking, think about this. At the times in my life when I was most alone I felt the least lonely, and in those moments, I discovered an appreciation for myself. I realized that I was the person I admired and wanted to be like.

I gave myself permission to be myself. I put away my need to be needed, and I stopped looking to others to fill me up. I started giving myself what I needed, and the loneliness went away.

It amazed me how when I felt like all of my needs were being met, no matter how alone I physically was; I was not at all lonely. The key is to satisfy all of your needs because if one is missing, the loneliness creeps back in. The problem for many of us is that we concentrate on our material needs and neglect our spiritual needs. That is when the loneliness is strongest of all.

I found that the more I gave myself permission to be myself, the more I came in contact with people like me. It was like they were just coming out of the woodwork, or perhaps it was just that I could finally see them.

Instead of trying to deny the qualities I disliked in myself and avoiding others who embodied them, I started embracing all of who I was and seeing the best in others. I realized that when I wasn't having the interesting conversations I desired, it was because I was not initiating them.

So my recommendation is, figure out who you are. Try new things and discover all the things you never knew about yourself. Tell the truth with your every action. If you don't feel like going out, don't go. If you would rather go to a museum than a nightclub, make the choice that will soothe your soul and reflect who you are as a person.

Finally, don't worry if you cannot find people to go on the journey with you. The whole point of the journey is to meet like-minded people along the way. The important thing is to be yourself, tell your truth, and by all means take the journey. I assure you, it will be thoroughly satisfying.

Action Plan: For Attracting What You Are

1. Discover who you are.
2. Take yourself on dates to learn what it is you truly enjoy doing.
3. Keep an open mind about yourself. You may discover things about yourself you never knew.
4. Be yourself and be true to whichever version of you happens to be present in that given moment.

If You Want to Know How He Feels About You, Ask Him, Then Listen

When I was sixteen, I had a male friend named Audi that told me something that stuck with me and helped me greatly as I navigated my way through the dating scene. He said, "A man will tell you exactly what he wants when he first meets you, and he very rarely changes his mind. The problem with women is they don't listen; they always think they can change us."

I was not sure at first if I should have believed him. I ran the words around in my head, looking for contradictory evidence to disprove his theory, but I couldn't find any. Then he accidentally and coincidentally proved his theory to me.

My friend Lacy had a crush on Audi, and she told pretty much everyone about it. When Audi found out he declared very clearly, "I don't like that girl."

One night, Lacy and I were spending the night at our friend Alex's house, and Audi happened to come by with his friend Mark. Audi was so mean and rude to Lacy; she ended up locking herself in the bathroom to cry. We made Audi go and coax her out so we could all play a game of Truth or Dare. I'm not sure what he said to her, but she happily came out of the bathroom to join us in the game.

Somewhere along the way, Truth or Dare did what it is known for doing and turned our innocent getting-to-know-you game into a make-out session. Alex was really close to both boys so she was excluded from the make-out aspect. Lacy and I ended up going into another room to make out with the boys. Lacy and Audi spent hours making out with each other as did Mark and I, and when the sun came up we realized we needed to hurry up and get those boys out of the house, before Alex's mom woke up.

I had a moment alone with Audi before they left and I asked him if he liked Lacy more after spending the night making out with her. His reply was, "No. I already told you I don't like her; that won't change just because she threw herself at me. Guys may make out with or even have sex with a girl, but if we didn't like her before we still won't like her after. You women have to learn how to listen and not let men take advantage of you thinking you can make them change."

That lesson kept me from making a lot of mistakes. I started hearing men differently when they spoke. If a guy walked by and told me he thought I was sexy, I did not mistake that for I want a relationship with you. I took it for what it was. I didn't misinterpret such crass statements as, "Hey let me hit that!" to be anything other than exactly what it was; and I did not get involved with men thinking I could change them. I had another problem altogether.

I was ridiculously shy and deathly afraid of rejection, so when it came to dealing with men, I would not make the first move, or the second, or the third. I would not voluntarily call a guy no matter how much I liked him, but I would return a call if he called me. This hindered me from pursuing the men I really liked and for the most part created a situation in which I only dated men who seemed to really like me.

That was not the extent of the problem. I not only refused to pursue men, I also had trouble telling them how I felt about them once we became involved, and I could not bring myself to ask them how they really felt about me even if my life depended on it. Most of the time, this left me feeling like I was in some kind of relationship purgatory. I would have these amazing interactions with men, but would be scared to move forward because I wasn't certain if what I was feeling was mutual or if I was projecting what I felt onto him. I became aware of it when my inability to speak freely caused me to lose a man that I really loved, more than one actually.

In retrospect, the very first time I became aware of how bad this problem was, I was already married. I was having a moment of insecurity, and I did not know how to tell my husband I needed some reassurance. I didn't know how to get him to express what he felt for me in a manner that would allay my doubt and allow me to rest easy, knowing that he really cared for me and that I had indeed made the right decision in marrying him.

In an effort to provoke him into saying what I wanted to hear, I asked him how he would feel about me becoming a stripper. I expected him to be adamantly and possessively against it. After all, what man would want his new wife to be a stripper? His reply threw me for a loop; he said, "Go ahead, we can use the money."

I was disconcerted; I had put my foot in my mouth trying to bait him, and he seemed not to care. I couldn't back down at that point so I restructured my objective and adopted a new goal. If he wouldn't admit that he cared then I had to make him feel what it would really be like.

The following Monday I went to a bar that had pay by the minute strippers behind a glass wall, and I auditioned. The audition only required me to strip down to my bra and panties, and let the manager check me for indications of drug use. Once he was satisfied that I had no track marks, he hired me on the spot and told me I could start the following week.

I was excited and apprehensive when I went home and told my husband what I had done. I wasn't sure how he would respond, even though he had encouraged it. I almost thought he would be delighted, but he wasn't. He became distant and cold. Now I was confused. I had only done what he told me I should do; what reason did he have to be mad at me?

He kept saying, "I can't believe you got naked for another man."

I assured him that was not the case. I told him I had only stripped to my underwear which was essentially no different than wearing a bathing suit on the beach. For some reason, he didn't believe me. That pissed me off because I had no reason to lie about the degree of my disrobing. In fact I didn't lie to him about anything, and if I were going to fabricate my story I would not have admitted to going to the audition in the first place, not what occurred once I arrived.

That whole situation put such a damper on our relationship that I later wished I had just had the courage to address my insecurity and ask him the questions I really wanted answered from the beginning. I also wished that he had told the truth about how he felt.

It wasn't until we were divorcing that he told me how hurt he was by that experience. At that point, I asked him why he suggested I do it. His reply was, "I thought it was what you wanted, and I didn't want to stand in the way of that." He also said he believed if he had told me how he really felt I would go behind his back and do it anyway and ultimately stop being so open and honest with him.

All of that ridiculousness could have been prevented if I had just asked him how he felt. Here, I offer you the advice I couldn't take. If you want to know how people feel about you, ask them. Then listen. Do not foolishly lead yourself to believe that you can change them or wear them down. Do not listen to what you *want* to hear while blocking out what they are *really* saying. Also, do not allow yourself to be used for the gratification of another in the hopes that one day they will come around.

Listening when a man tells you his intentions instead of convincing yourself that you can change his mind is liberating. It allows your heart and mind to be free of Mr. Wrong so you can be fully available for Mr. Right when he comes along. Also, just so you know, if a man is disguising his intentions, chances are they are not pure, and he is not the right person for you. In a situation like this the best thing to do is see what you are being, to attract what you're attracting.

Action Plan: For Listening

1. When a man first approaches you pay attention to the words he uses; if they indicate that his intentions are not in line with what you want, DO NOT pursue further contact.
2. If you initiate contact, with a man be clear about what your intentions are and follow through with your actions.

3. If you find yourself in the company of a man or men who are in any way disrespecting you, leave. It likely will not end well if you stay.

4. When in doubt, ask a man you trust for his objective opinion; if he cares about you he will tell you the truth. LISTEN.

9

If She's Asking for Chocolate, Don't Give her Peanut Butter

This is what I told my best friend when she called one day asking for advice about her marriage. She said that she was doing everything she could to please her husband, and nothing she did was good enough. He was always complaining and unsatisfied.

My friend is a stay-at-home mother of two, and the degree to which her husband works outside of the home to provide for the family is the same degree to which she works inside the home trying to make it a pleasant and nurturing place for her family to live, love, and grow. It was the desire for these things that brought her to me. She could not understand what more she could do to make her husband happy.

The first thing I did was to simply ask her, "What did he say is wrong? What did he say he wanted?"

She began to tell me, "Well, he said he wanted the house clean when he came home from work, but he doesn't

74

understand that I spend the whole day cleaning the house; scrubbing the base boards, wiping the windowsills and disinfecting the floor, in addition to taking care of the kids. He just doesn't know how hard I work. When he comes home, if there's a pile of toys on the floor or dishes in the sink, he looks at me like I haven't done anything all day."

"Then at night," she continued, "he wants to have sex, but I am worn out from working in the house all day. I don't have the energy to have sex, and he doesn't want to help out around the house because he just went to work all day, and he feels like his job is done, and now is his time to rest. I mean that is understandable, but what about me?"

"I need a time to rest too. I don't ever get to rest. My work is never done; the kids are always making messes that need to be cleaned up, or I have to cook and feed them or bathe them. My job is non-stop; at least when he clocks out, his job ends. He just doesn't get it. I just don't know what to do."

"I see your dilemma," I told her. "You and your husband value different things. You value sanitation, and he values appearance. You want a deep down disinfected clean, and he wants neatness, or the appearance of clean. The truth is, you can spend the entire month sanitizing every inch of your home, but if it doesn't appear neat, and tidy when he walks through the door he will not recognize or acknowledge that you have done anything. I understand that you are doing what you believe to be in the best interest of your family, but what I am going to suggest is that you do what is in the best interest of your happiness and your marriage."

Quite simply, what I am saying is give the man what he wants. Using my friend's scenario as an example; focus your energy first on making the home *appear* neat and tidy. After that is complete, if you have time and energy to spare, work in small sections on sanitizing the place being careful not to overdo it or burn yourself out. When he comes home to a house that appears clean, he will be in a much better mood.

With his improved state of mind, it will be easier to engage him in assisting you, because he will see what he perceives to be evidence of what you did all day. If at that point you ask him to spend some time with the kids to give you a break while you prepare the evening meal, or take a shower, or whatever you need to do, he will be more than happy to oblige you because he will already have what he most needed-a comfortable place to sit down, relax, and let go of the stresses of the day. He will have room to breathe.

With this new, mutually beneficial, symbiotic relationship, you two will feel less frustration and resentment towards each other, and likely engage in more sexual activity. Note: the more sex you give him, the more he will want to do for you. The more he does for you, the more time and energy you will have to give him sex as well as give to yourself what you need. Life is a cycle. It can be a cycle of giving or taking, and you are the one that determines what your life is by your first action. That is to say, if you give first, he will give back, and you will have a cycle of giving, but if you take first, then he will take back, and you will have a cycle of taking.

Please understand, and this is very important, when giving you must be sure to give the other person what they want, not what you want.

As humans, we have a tendency to think that all of our personal likes and dislikes are the same as or better than those of others, so we tend to give the things we want and wonder why it goes unappreciated. One of the keys to building a strong relationship is communication. The biggest part of communication is listening. So when the person with whom you are in a relationship tells you what they want, listen and give them what they ask for. Otherwise, they may never recognize that they have been given anything at all.

For example, if your favorite snack is chocolate and your spouse loves peanut butter, do not delude yourself into believing you have done this amazing self-sacrificing thing by sharing with him your favorite chocolate. Yes, he will take the chocolate and eat it and maybe even thank you, but he will not appreciate it the way you expect him to. Likewise, when he goes looking for something to get you as a gift, he will give you peanut butter so you can see how good it is, and you will have a similar response.

What you create by doing this is a circle of discontent. You both appreciate the other's effort, but neither of you are feeling satisfied. If, on the other hand, you recognize his love for peanut butter, and you give him his favorite peanut butter as a reward, or dessert, or token of appreciation, he will be so grateful, fulfilled, and satisfied that he will return the favor by giving you your favorite chocolate.

Mind you, chocolate and peanut butter can be anything that the other person desires. They can represent a clean house versus a sanitized house, or oral sex versus vaginal sex, or going to the movies versus going to the game. The key is to find out what your partner's desires are, and give it to him or her without expectation, simply out of love for that person, and a desire to see them happy. This is another very important point to recognize. If you act with the expectation that your actions will be reciprocated you are setting yourself up for the possibility of disappointment. You have to act selflessly and without expectation.

Here's the thing; reciprocity is a guarantee. The problem, however, is that it may not happen immediately. He may be stuck in a rut on the cycle the two of you have been on for the past few years, and he may take longer to come off of it than you do. As long as you keep working to change the cycle, it will eventually change.

It's like water in a tub; if you stick your hand in the water and rotate it in a circle, the water will begin to flow in a circular motion in the direction of your hand. If you later want to change the direction of the water you have to stick your hand in the water and turn it in the opposite direction. The water will not immediately change. You will meet with some resistance, and for a few cycles the water will be going against you, but eventually, with a bit of persistence, the cycle of the water will completely change and begin to flow in the direction of your hand. The same is true of your relationship.

If you begin living and acting in the direction you would like your relationship to go, it will eventually catch up. You may initially feel like it's not working, and you may even come up against a little resistance, but if you just keep moving in that direction, the law of reciprocity dictates that your relationship, and whatever other aspects of your life you are working on, will eventually fall in line."

This advice works for most relationships, not just marriages, and in other aspects of life as well. Please apply it liberally wherever you see it can be useful in your life.

Action Plan: For Getting What You Want

1. Get to know the people you are involved with as *they* are; not how you want them to be.
2. Make a concerted daily effort to give them at least one thing that brings them joy.
3. Allow them to get to know you as you *really* are, not the person you felt you needed to be to get them.

4. Ask for what you want. The Bible in Matthew chapter 7 gives the best advice in this regard. It says <u>keep</u> on asking and it will be given to you. If this is true of God, it is safe to assume that with men it would be all the more so.

10

If You Want to Spend More Time With Him, Don't Buy Him a Play-Station

As Christmas was approaching, everyone I knew was scurrying to find gifts for the ones they loved. I had one friend call me to tell me she was considering getting her husband the latest version of the play station.

Before I could stop myself, the words "DON'T DO THAT" blasted forth from my mouth. My reaction was so strong she was momentarily taken aback. "Oh my gosh." she said, "You feel very strong about that, why do you say that?"

I then shared with her the flood of memories that came rushing back to my mind and out of my lips in that one emphatic statement. Memories that were so deeply repressed, I was not even aware that they still affected me. Memories so intense, they prompted me to not only share them with her but also with anyone who could be helped by them, because apparently they were so deeply rooted that the only way to truly release them was to use them as an informative tool from which others could hopefully learn.

For me, it started about seven months into my marriage. I was already pregnant, and my husband had been working at his job for a few months and was beginning to acquaint himself with his co-workers. It did not take him long to discover that one of his co-workers lived in the same apartment complex as we did. Not only that, but this particular friend had a shared interest in video games and owned the latest one made by Sony called the Play-Station.

This man who we will call A.J. invited my husband over to play the Play-Station with him one night, and to my chagrin, my husband ended up staying there until the wee hours of the morning. The only thing I found more upsetting was that it soon became a regular thing with them.

As it was, my husband didn't get off work until ten or eleven o'clock at night, and to have him come home, only to leave right back out to his friend's house to play the Play-Station was disconcerting. It seemed no matter what I had going on, there was something going on in the video game community that was more pressing. If I was planning a romantic dinner for two, they were having a tournament, which trumped my plans by far.

When we moved out of that complex I thought it was going to put an end to all of this Play-Station nonsense and keep my husband home more. What it actually did was keep him out of the house more because now he had to leave the complex to go to his friends' house and was reluctant to come right back to assuage my feelings or tend to my needs. I was too far away for him to temporarily leave the party and go right back, so he just disregarded me and stayed there with A.J.

Thinking that I was "smarter than the average bear," I decided to buy my husband a Play-Station for our one-year anniversary in an effort to make our home a more attractive place for him to be. I thought if he had the same gaming system at home he would be more likely to stay home. I thought he might from time to time invite his friends over to play it with him, but that was a burden I was willing to endure to keep him home more. I even believed that I would play it with him, and it would somehow bring us closer together.

What I learned is that those video games are way more addictive than I could have anticipated, and I had no interest in them. My husband did play his frequently when he was home. However, he did not stay home only to play it. In fact, he basically just used it as a tool to improve his skill level so that he would be better equipped to win more often when competing with his friends in their tournaments.

This essentially had the effect of giving us less time together. I wanted him to spend less time with his friends and more time at home. What I got was a husband who spent the same amount of time with his friends and less time with me while he was at home. Instead of the little bit of quality time I had complained about, I was put even further on the back burner while he played the video game I almost immediately regretted buying him.

The lesson I learned from that experience dealt with manipulation and control. I was trying to use my spouse's passion to control him and manipulate him into staying home, and spending time with me. Clearly it backfired; not only did I not get what I wanted, but I got even more of what I didn't want.

I cautioned my friend, "Learn from my mistake." I told her, "If you want to spend more time with your husband then make arrangements to do things you both enjoy doing together, and make sure you tell him well in advance so he will be sure to show up."

It is important to note here that you get what you want by creating opportunities for you to get what you want. If you focus on what you fear, you inevitably invite your fears into your life as I did. Do not do what I did. Focus your attention on your actual desire and not what you believe to be standing in the way of it.

When you are planning activities to spend time with your significant other, make an effort to find things to do outside of the house. If you are on a budget, do free or inexpensive things like going to the park, an art show, or a comedy club on open mic night when it's usually free. Discover your interests, and seek venues that offer discounted prices on particular days or times of day. What you do is not as important as leaving the house to do it.

Leaving the house is fundamentally important because this type of man ~ the kind who won't stay home and spend quality time ~ views being in the house as inactivity. He doesn't comprehend quality time, so when he asks you what you want to do, and you tell him you're preparing dinner for the two of you, what he hears is, "Nothing important but dinner will be ready whenever you get here." He appreciates that you cooked but sees no urgency in coming home. There is no deadline or urgency; it's just dinner.

However, if you tell him you made plans to go somewhere, even if it is just to listen to jazz in the park, he will know that there is a scheduled time for your date and will feel like not making it a priority will disappoint you. He will make a greater effort.

Curiously this works for the other type of man as well. The one who believes he is spending quality time with you, because he is home every night. The biggest complaint with him is that he won't leave the house to take you out. Well scheduling plans works just as well on him. You just have to tell him your plans well in advance.

This last bit of advice is extremely important and it applies to both types. <u>Follow through no matter what</u>. If you make plans, make sure it is to do something you enjoy doing anyway. When the time comes, get dressed up and leave whether he agrees to accompany you or not, whether he is even home or not.

For the guy who prefers to stay home, he will see you getting dressed and be curious about your intentions. He will at first believe that if he doesn't go, you will change your mind and stay home with him. Don't. If you leave him a couple of times, he is going to begin to wonder what is drawing your attention away from him. He will begin to accompany you if for no other reason than curiosity. If he enjoys himself while out, it will be less difficult to get him to go next time. Also consider doing something with a regular schedule for this type of man, as he tends to be more comfortable with structured arrangements. You can vary the event and keep the days of the week the same perhaps.

For the other type ~ the one who likes to be out ~ if he comes home on time, it is to go with you. Problem solved. If for some reason he doesn't get home on time, disregard his excuses and leave without him. Again make sure you are dressed up for the occasion. When he does arrive and sees you missing, his curiosity will either prompt him to go meet you or keep him home awaiting your return. When you get home all dressed up looking like you had a good time, he will feel like he missed out on something. He will not ever want to feel that way again. Next time, he will go with you.

I know it sounds like you have to play a lot of games to get what you want, and to some degree, it can feel like that.

What you are really doing though is you giving yourself what you want, and the man is stepping up to meet you where you are. You have to do for yourself regardless of him, and when you do he will join you so that you don't move on without him. That is assuming of course he truly loves you and wants to be with you.

Do not get discouraged if this doesn't work the first few times. Remember change is a slow process. Just keep in mind that you are doing what you desire to do, and if at some point you want to do something different, then do that too. The key here is to know yourself and give yourself what you need instead of trying to manipulate someone else into giving you what you want.

Action Plan: For Getting More Time

1. Inform your significant other of your desires.
2. Make concrete plans and give your partner advanced notice of your intentions.
3. Only make plans to do things you will enjoy
4. Stick to your plans. Barring an actual emergency this step is crucial.
5. Be consistent.

Do Not Ask Questions You Don't Want The Answer To

Honesty and forthrightness are what we claim to want, but sometimes we really can't handle the truth. I will here caution you; be careful what you ask for, because you just might get it.

We don't truly appreciate how blissful ignorance can be until we have to deal with reality. For those who are prepared to handle any possibility, I encourage you go forth in the direction of truth. However, for my more fragile readers, I implore you to be as steadfast as a military soldier; don't ask your partner to tell you a truth you may not be ready to hear.

When I was dating the man I later married, there was a point at which I felt the need to ascertain the seriousness of our relationship. I was not sure if we were exclusive yet, but I thought I wanted us to be. While we were out on a date one evening, I asked him if he had been with any other women since we started dating. When he said "yes," my heart dove into my stomach and collapsed my lung along the way. It took me a moment to catch my breath.

I was devastated by his response, but what could I do? I had asked the question, and he answered honestly. I thanked him for being truthful, and then berated myself for asking questions I did not want the answer to. I learned that day that sometimes it feels better to not know, but I am the type who prefers to make informed decisions. I would choose knowing over not knowing any day.

Some years later when we were married, my best friend from high school and her boyfriend came to visit us for a week. It was a rare occasion where she had time off work that fit into all of our schedules. While she and I caught up and reminisced on old times, my husband took her boyfriend and showed him around the city. They told us they were going to play basketball, but there really is no telling what all they got into. When they returned from one of their daily outings, my husband asked to speak to me privately.

We inconspicuously disappeared into the bedroom, and he asked me if my friend knew that her boyfriend was married. I sincerely doubted it, but I was also not inclined to be presumptuous. I told him I would find out, and if she didn't know I would tell her. I thanked him for bringing it to my attention, and we rejoined them.

I did not bring up the marriage issue until the next day when we were again left alone to spend time together. By this time I had undergone some sensitivity training and remembered how it felt to find out information I did not necessarily want to have. So before blurting out to my friend "Hey your boyfriend is married to another woman," I decided to ask her if she would want to know.

I was surprised when she told me she would not like me to share with her any information I may have had regarding her boyfriend. She confided in me that other people had already told her all types of rumors about him including, but not limited to, him being married. She said when she asked him about it he told her it wasn't true, and she had chosen to believe him. I respected her wishes and kept my information to myself.

I did wonder though why he would tell my husband he was married and tell her he wasn't as if it wouldn't get back to her. I also wondered about her ostrich approach to life. I mean, we lived in two different states on opposite sides of the country. I had only just met him for the first time, and Myspace and Facebook had not yet been invented. Common sense should have told her that the only way I could have acquired such information was if it came directly from him. Still, I respected her choice. I knew how awful it could feel to be showered with painful information before you were ready for it.

I understood that everyone had to deal with the issues present in their life in their own way, and just because we had different ways of dealing with things, it did not make one method superior to the other. I got a glimpse then of how inclined we are as women to deny our instincts for the preservation of our relationships.

Some years later, a married man, who was looking to have an extramarital affair, approached me. I expressed to this man, who thought he was getting away with cheating on his wife, just because she hadn't caught him in the act didn't mean she was unaware of what was going on. Women are embedded with intuitive instincts that tell us when something is askew in our relationships. We may not ask, and we may not act on it because we may have learned the hard way not to ask until we're ready to know, but the fact remains, instinctively we always know.

He argued with me telling me that if she knew, she would have left him a long time ago. "Not necessarily," I told him. "I am sure she is smarter than that. She may not be ready to venture off into the world alone and fend for herself. She may be biding her time and stacking her chips until her safety net is of satisfactory size. She may be cheating as well and feel content that so long as you are doing it you won't catch onto her. She also could have decided to just forgive you and remain as true to her vows as she could, recognizing that at some point you will have to answer for your sins, as she will have to answer for hers. The only thing I can absolutely guarantee you regarding the reason she is staying, is that it is not because she doesn't know."

Not asking is not the same as not knowing. It is just a good way to put off dealing with what you inherently know for as long as you can. So if you think there is a possibility that receiving an answer other than the one you are looking for will cause you more distress then you are ready to handle, then by all means do not ask the question.

Action Plan: For Seeking Information

1. Do not ask questions you don't want the answer to.
2. Trust your instincts and your intuition. They will always tell you what you need to know if you listen.
3. Evaluate the motives of others before accepting their opinions about your relationship.

Happily Ever After Doesn't Just Happen

Family is such a tricky and fickle thing. We are born of people who may or may not want us, and they treat us according to the circumstances and purposes pertaining to and/or surrounding our conception. These people, who we call our parents, are the first examples we have of this entity called family. Once outside of our mothers' womb, family tends to take on a variety of appearances.

Some people do not ever learn to view the people who gave them life as family, and for others, those two people are the only family they ever know. When the people who created you create more children, they become your family as well, and this unit composes what we typically call an immediate family.

An immediate family does not have to consist of birth parents and their offspring. It need only have one or more parental guardians exercising jurisdiction over one or more children who consider themselves siblings. They could be adopted, step, half, or whole siblings, and that has no bearing whatsoever on their commitment to each other.

After immediate family comes extended family; this includes but is not limited to aunts, uncles, cousins, grandparents, nieces, nephews, and in-laws.

Then, there is the family we create for ourselves, which includes play cousins, boyfriends, girlfriends, best friends, God-parents, and any other person who falls in the friendship category and hangs around so long you stop trying to send them away.

Sometimes we grow closer to our extended family than we are to our immediate family, and for some of us, an extended family is all we have left. A lot of people value the family they create for themselves over the biological one, asserting that somehow, because it is by choice, it is more meaningful.

These unique dynamics are what make family so desirable and so fickle. It is nice for us as humans to think that we have someone in our corner who is there for us, backing us up no matter what we do or how foolish we may be.

We want to know that there are people out there who are not judging us, just loving us. We need to feel that, in spite of our imperfections, we are still capable of receiving love. Most importantly perhaps, we would like to believe that there exists in this world at least one other person who can follow our train of thought and possibly even understand it.

That's what is so interesting about the relationships

between parents and children as well as siblings. The love shared in these unions comes the closest to being unconditional that can be found in present day society. Oftentimes the parents don't even have the same level of love and commitment for each other.

In its portrayal of love, television does not accurately convey how difficult it can be for two people with different upbringings, and backgrounds, to try and merge their lives. It's sad that the way in which our immediate family raised us is what we come to associate with love, for better or worse. Though we may tolerate more injurious behaviors from the people we give our love to, we also tend to expect more from them.

It is not uncommon in new relationships, for people to increase their expectations when they realize they're in love. In family, love allows for acceptance without expectation, but in relationships, not only do the expectations change once a commitment is established, but sometimes there is a desire on the part of one partner to completely change the person they now love into the person they believe they should be with in their mind.

This creates conflict in relationships, because as I mentioned before, people do not want to have to change for love. They want the same kind of unconditional acceptance they received from their other family units. They want to be marveled at for the things that make them different, instead of molded into a cookie cutter cast of the same old thing. They want to be understood on a deeper level, and that kind of understanding cannot come from someone who can't see past the changes they want to create.

New relationships are hard, and turning these new relationships into family units is harder still. In youth the degree of difficulty is lower. There are fewer expectations and demands. Young people have little knowledge of what the picture of the budding relationship should look like. And the getting to know you process is different, because as youths we are also still getting to know ourselves.

In youth, as we learn who we are, we tend to share what we learn with whomever happens to be in our life at the time. If there is are people we have relationships with, we divulge all of our innermost secrets to them, and they come to know us as we know ourselves, and they accept us for whom we are because their expectations are low. There is a connection, an attraction, and now a bond. If one person does not severely hurt the other, this relationship can last a long time.

The biggest problem that stems from these types of relationships is societies' influence telling the people involved in them that they are missing out on something by not exploring whatever else may be out there. Too often people, particularly men, will buy into this notion that being with one person for your whole life is not significant and is not enough. They are highly pressured to get out of this comfortable created family and explore other options.

They seldom find again what they had at first, but they rarely seem to know that for sure. What happens is, when they look back at what they gave up, they do not feel bad because it no longer looks appealing. They see a person who has changed in ways they never thought possible, and they don't stop to think about the way in which they created the change they see.

As we live, grow, and go in and out of relationships, it becomes more and more difficult to achieve that family unit we all desperately want. We forget how, or choose not to open up and share ourselves with the people in our lives, for fear that they will somehow use this information against us. Another fear is that this will just be another failed relationship we have invested too much time and energy into.

We begin to stop the process before it even starts, or sabotage it somewhere in the middle. This process is further complicated as we get older, by every experience we have and witness along the way. All of life's negative aspects that we carry with us into this new situation decrease its chances of success. Baggage, babies, and a maligned attitude toward the opposite sex due to a previous betrayal; there is no end to the reasons it may not work.

Nobody wants to deal with and work through these obstacles, but everybody has them. In the event that you do find a person that you like enough to try to work through the surface issues with, the question then becomes, how do we merge our lives? With the divorce rate so high, this question begs the more pressing question, do we even want to? But how can you be a family without merging lives? It just grows more and more complicated until, at some point, you either give up, or you figure it out and pray for the miracle it will require for it to work.

Child rearing is another area in which adults complicate their relationships. With the escalating divorce rate, single parenting is more prevalent now than at any other period in recorded history. When approaching the prospect of a relationship with a single parent, we spend way too much time over-thinking the dynamics and not enough time just allowing what can happen quite naturally to just happen. As adults, we tend to forget that children are people too, and we underestimate their intelligence. We sometimes attempt to hide things from them thinking we are protecting them, and often they see more, or know more about what's going on than we do.

We also tend to forget that above all else, children want to be happy. As much as they want to see mom and dad together, listening to mom and dad scream at each other does not make for a happy child. It is often the case that our children would prefer us to find happiness with someone new, than exist miserably together for the sake of remaining a family.

Do not misunderstand, I am in no way suggesting that divorce is the better option; I am only mentioning a possible child's perspective. However, though children know and understand so much more than we give them credit for, they are still children, and they therefore do not know or understand everything, especially pertaining to adult relationships. They are still taking their cues from us, so they will know how to behave when they get into their own relationships.

I believe in marriage, and the family unit, and I personally advocate keeping the family together whenever possible. However, I also realize the cost at which this scenario may sometimes come. Staying together requires a quality that we all want other people to have, but that we ourselves do not necessarily exercise. It requires forgiveness. The same kind we ask of God when we sin, the same kind we gave our parents growing up when they caused us harm, and the same kind we expect, and receive from our children, as we do things that are occasionally less than beneficial to them.

We as people all make mistakes, and we all fall short, but in relationships when it comes to forgiving, we are much better receivers than givers. I once heard it said, "A good relationship is made up of two very good forgivers." I immediately recognized the truth in that, and I held onto it because I thought that was all it would take to carry me through in my own marriage. What I learned from my marriage though is that while being a good forgiver is essential to the longevity of the relationship, it is not the only requirement.

Both partners also need to be more lovingly selfish, putting their own needs before all others. The law of reciprocity dictates that what you put out will come back to you. If you consider this in making the choices that are in your own best interest, you will do fewer things that need to be forgiven.

I witnessed the effects of the universal law of reciprocity first hand in my marriage. I did a great many things that required my husband's forgiveness, and the things he did were definitely one way in which those things came right on back around to me. The thing about reciprocity is that, once you put something out there, you never know in what form it will return, which is all the more reason ~ out of love for yourself ~ to be careful what you do to others.

The problem I encountered in my own personal experience was that, though I was capable of forgiving my partner for a great many indiscretions, I had no interest in allowing him to endanger my life. I enjoy life way too much, and have too much to live for. When things were done that I felt compromised me to the point where I discerned a lack of concern for the quality or continuance of my life, I chose to forgive him and move on.

I know that everyone's situations, reasons, and strengths are different, and sometime it's just a little thing that festers and drives a huge wedge between two people; to the point where they can no longer stand to be in each others presence, but if the lines of honest communication can be opened long enough to resolve the issue, then preservation can occur. But please, do not expect this process to be easy.

Relationships take work, and that too is something we tend to forget. We have no qualms about working to make money, or to acquire any other material possession our heart desires, but for an intangible item like love, we do not want to work. We convince ourselves that the television is accurate in its portrayal of how people meet, instantly fall in love, and live happily ever after. Then, if ever after is not so happy, they split up and find somebody new.

We don't even want to do the work required of us for our own happiness. We look for people to complete us and make us whole instead of making ourselves whole and finding a person who will compliment who we are. We tend to not enjoy our own company and then get upset when we no longer enjoy the company of another. We as people tend to demand more of others than we do of ourselves.

We have a "take me as I am, and by the way can you change please" mentality. There is nothing healthy in the way we approach relationships today, but as I mentioned before, we got our examples from our parents, who changed society but did not know how to adjust to the changes they made.

The world was changing, and the strain it was putting on

relationships grew unbearable for the people in them, so they gave up, and that became our life lesson. The dynamics between men and women also changed, to the effect that women needed to be stronger, and men felt more comfortable bailing. Societal changes created familial changes, which caused an overabundance of dysfunctional people.

Now we want these dysfunctional people to figure out how to re-create family structures. Tell me that isn't asking a lot. Not to say that it can't be done, but in the midst of the 'me', and 'me now' generations, I would just like to ask, who is going to do it? Who is going to stand up and say "okay enough about me, what about the family?" What media personnel is going to flood the airwaves with shows about what reality should be, instead of the extremes of what reality is currently? If change had a hope of occurring, where would it come from, and what happens if it doesn't? Imagine what the world would be without family... Scary, isn't it?

So, let's be the change we want to see. Let us do the work. Let us communicate and work through the problems instead of bailing when it seems a little too hard, or someone more interesting comes along. The grass is not always greener on the other side, and even when it is, in the age of genetic modification, you don't know what made it that way.

Yes, it will be hard to find people we want to be with and try to make something good come out of it. So let's start with the people who are already together. Let us help them work on staying together. Let's stop trying to mislead them into believing that leaving is better. Let us stop trying to tempt them to be unfaithful to the person they are with. Let us encourage instead of discouraging unions and find ways to make people feel good regarding the choices they have made. Let us stop making excuses for those who leave and justifying it as if it were normal or right. Let us learn how to do more talking and less hitting. Let us look inside to our partner and not outside of our relationships for the things we believe will fulfill us. Let's stop putting people on a pedestal and waiting for them to fall off of it. We are all human, we are all imperfect, we all make mistakes, we all fall short, and we all seek forgiveness, so we should all give it.

That is not to say that there are not some circumstances where a parting of ways needs to occur, it's just to say that phrases such as irreconcilable differences should not be allowed in our vocabulary where family is concerned. In my opinion, irreconcilable differences is code for, I am too lazy to try anymore, or I think there is something better out there.

WAKE UP PEOPLE! There is nothing better anywhere. Everything is what you make it, and what appears to be better is really a façade. We have all seen movie sets that clearly shows what appears to be a house, is really just some painted cardboard on concrete with furniture strategically placed around it. Everything in this society fits the same pattern, so why are we buying into it?

Why do we believe that reality TV is reality? Why do we believe that fast food is real food? Why do we believe that the president is fit to represent the country? None of these things make sense, and neither does ending a relationship due to communication differences. We need to stop walking away and evolve, learn how to communicate, and be willing to grow. I wish everybody would just stop for two seconds, to have an original thought, and then let that two seconds multiply, until we are spending minutes, and then hours thinking for ourselves.

It is a really liberating experience. Once it is mastered, original thought liberates us from the confines of other people's opinions. Not only that, but it aids in the process of self-discovery and allows true purpose and desire to be laid bare.

It is at this point that we discover that not everything is as it appears to be, and the other side is not as happy as we could be right where we are. All of this is just food for thought, and I am only telling you these things because I love you.

So now let us go out and learn something new, learn how to love ourselves, and then try learning to love the ones we're with. If we master that, then we can love the people around us, and when we collectively get to that point, the whole world can change. No worries though; it's baby steps.

Action Plan: For Happily Ever After

1. Change the way you look at marriage. See it much like the career of your dreams. Yes, it's work, but it's the work you love to do.

2. Recognize that it's not going to be perfect at first but as with everything else in life with enough practice you can achieve perfection.

3. Continuously get to know the person you married. He or she is changing just as you are. Change is the only constant in this world.

4. Share the things you learn and your evolving interests. Grow together so you don't grow apart.

Part 3

Obvious Truths about Parenting

Insanity is hereditary; you get it from your children.

-Sam Levenson

If the child is Quiet
Leave the Cornflakes on the Floor

The hardest thing about being a new mother is finding a moment to rest when the child is not screaming, crying, or vying for your attention. The second hardest thing is getting the father to contribute more to the parenting. One solution, for the latter, is creating situations in which the father has no choice but to be responsible for the care of the child. However, when you as a mother make the choice to leave your child in the care of its father, it is important to know that his care giving is not likely to resemble your own.

I learned this the hard way. After my son was born, I got burnt out with the responsibility of having a job, going to school, and having a new baby. As a result I ended up losing my job, and putting school on hold, so I could focus on my baby. I got a job as a school bus driver so I could earn enough money to cover my expenses and have the majority of my day to spend with my son.

This meant that his father was caring for him in the mornings while I was out working. One day, I returned home from work to find my living room floor covered in corn flakes and my son sitting in my husbands lap, watching him play the play-station. My initial reaction was outrage. I was furious that he would just leave the mess in the middle of the floor, sit down, and play video games, as if nothing was wrong. I assumed that he was expecting me to come home and clean up the mess that he allowed our child to make.

I was not in the mood to clean up any messes I didn't make or allow to happen. So, to offset what I assumed were his expectations, I began yelling and fussing about the mess. I ranted and raved about his negligence, and all the bugs that leaving food on the floor would likely attract. He got defensive and started yelling back at me about what a hard time he had trying to get our son to settle down and be quiet. Then, our son joined the chaos and started screaming, crying, and reaching for me.

Now I had an irritated husband, a crying clingy child, and a living room that looked like it had been hit by a natural disaster. I had just turned what at first glance appeared to be a bad situation into my own personal hell. I did this by overreacting to a situation without knowing all of the facts. I learned from my mistake.

A few years later, when a friend called me upset that every time she left her daughter home alone with her father, the house was a mess, and the baby appeared uncared for, I gave her the best advice I could. I told her quite simply, "If the child is quiet, leave the corn flakes on the floor."

She did not at first understand my analogy because her situation involved toys and clothes, not corn flakes, but I told her the same theory applies. We as mothers, spend more time nesting and preparing for the arrivals of our babies than our non-pregnant partners. Then after the babies arrive we spend more time caring for them on a regular basis. It is foolish of us, to assume that our partners would be as adept at taking care of them as we are, when they have so little training and opportunity.

The only way to increase the efficiency with which a man cares for his child, is to give him more opportunities to do so. That includes allowing him to clean up the messes he permits the baby to make. If he never gets an opportunity to do the work, he never learns to appreciate how much work is involved. He therefore assumes that it's as easy as we mothers learn to make it look.

He also begins to rely on you and seek you out to clean up whatever mess he allows the baby to make. This was the outcome I was trying to avoid with the corn flakes situation, when I went in the house yelling and screaming; which I quickly discovered was also not the right approach. I know that now because, though it had the intended affect of making him clean up the cornflakes, I had created a much bigger emotional mess.

What I should have done, what I learned to do, and what I now advise other women to do, is learn to leave things be. When you walk in the door and see the corn flakes on the floor, just peak around to make sure the baby is quiet and ok, and then leave before they notice you're there. You can go back out and treat yourself to something special, like a cup of coffee, or go back to bed, or find something that you have been meaning to get done to make yourself look busy. That way when they do realize you're there, their first impulse will not be to put you to work.

This will do two things. One it will give you the break you so desperately need, and two, it will help him learn how to do things for the baby by himself. The key is to make sure when the baby starts to stir and become unmanageable again, you either are unavailable leaving him to handle it all on his own, or you take the baby, and allow him to clean up the mess, and then give him the baby back immediately. The challenge will be that once he cleans up the mess, he will try to leave, claiming he has something really important to do.

Over time, you will learn to either create more really important things for you to do so that he can grow as a father, or stop complaining about all the things he doesn't do realizing that you enable the situation because it is what you prefer. There is nothing wrong with being a control freak that wants to be needed all the time, but if that is who you are, then just acknowledge it and stop complaining about it. Embrace who you are, and be proud of it knowing that you have the power to change it at any time.

Another very wise thing to do, in the training process of getting your partner to be an efficient parent, is to compliment him on the progress he makes. If, for instance, he finally figures out how to make the bottle while holding the baby, be sure to give him a kiss and tell him what a good job he is doing without sounding condescending. This will inspire him to want to do even more things better.

People need praise, and just as we mothers truly want nothing more than to be appreciated for the hard work and effort we exhaust in raising our family, our partners want to be recognized and raved over for their contributions as well.

So maybe he can't change a diaper without leaving the baby unattended, or rock the baby to sleep while cooking dinner. He still wants to be acknowledged for trying. If given enough opportunities and adulation, he just may surprise you and clean up the corn flakes before you get home next time.

Don't get too excited. He will still be sitting there letting the baby watch him, while he plays the video game, but they will both be quiet, and the house will appear clean. Hey, progress is a slow process, but still it is progress.

Action Plan: For Getting What You Need

1. Pray, and trust God to protect your child when leaving him or her with someone else.
2. Realize there is a learning curve. Not everyone will be as adept at taking care of your child as you are, but with practice, they can be.
3. Offer praise for any effort or improvement you see, and look for things to take notice of.

14

If I Can't Sleep Nobody Can

Babies are nondiscriminatory in demanding that their needs are met. When they are hungry, they cry. When they are wet, or otherwise uncomfortable, they cry. When they are sleepy, or filled with gas they cry, and cry, and cry, getting increasingly louder until the problem is addressed. They might, if they were capable, meet these needs themselves, but as they do not have the skills yet to do so, they are steadfast and resolute in using the skills they do have, to make sure that their needs are addressed.

I find that people who take this approach to life are also successful at getting their needs met. I used to believe that being uncompromising and demanding was a selfish and abominable characteristic. I considered my husband and all of my closest friends to have this quality, and I could not figure out why I was attracting all of these selfish people to me.

From my perspective, I was not selfish. I was retaliatory which, in retrospect, may have been worse, but back then I thought it was completely justifiable. I made myself always available to anybody who might need me and resented my friends when they didn't answer their phone or respond to my outreach. I found it hurtful when they were so consumed with their own lives that they did not even take the time to see if perhaps what I wanted was important enough to lend their attention. They just put me on the back burner, assuming I would still be there when they needed me again, and guess what? I was. Why should they believe anything different if I was proving them right?

Being such a great friend made me an awful spouse, and I couldn't even see it. I was so busy complaining about how my husband was neglecting my needs by putting his friends first, I couldn't see that I was doing the exact same thing. I was so available to my friends and family that if they called in the middle of sex, I would answer the phone. I wouldn't stop having sex to talk to them, but I would definitely answer the phone just to make sure everything was okay. In some cases I would even talk for a few minutes while having sex. I considered myself to be excellent at multi-tasking.

They considered me to be crazy. They all thought it was funny, that I was capable and willing to do so many things at once. My husband was less impressed. He started feeling neglected and unimportant, and no matter how much I tried to tell him that was not the case, my actions were shouting something else. In the entire time we were married I never realized the effect those actions had on him.

He complained frequently that I ignored him and put other people before him, but I was always there. Sure, I would be on the phone for hours, but at least I was at home. He was always leaving me to go hang out with his friends, or go assist them with whatever minor crisis was more pressing than what I wanted to do, and I wondered daily how I ended up with such a selfish man. It's almost as if I was blind to my own behavior, but everything the people close to me did was like a smite to my ego.

I recall a time when he came home drunk at four in the morning, and I wanted to talk. He was so exhausted from partying that the last thing he wanted to do was talk. Try as I may; I could not get him to stay awake long enough to have a conversation with me about how he made me feel by leaving me and staying out all night. I couldn't sleep because I was consumed by my own emotions and the desire to express them, so I determined that he should experience what I was experiencing.

I did everything I could to make it impossible for him to sleep. I would scratch him with my toenails, or hit him with my elbows while pretending to roll over, all to no avail. Even if I woke him, he would not stay awake to talk. When those antics failed, I resorted to even more ludicrous behavior.

I would get up and turn on every appliance in the house. I would turn the radio up full blast and put it on an AM station with nothing but static, and then I would turn on the television to full volume and disconnect the cable wire so all he could here was more static, and then I would turn on every light in the house, and get back in the bed, and lay there as if I were trying to sleep.

He would wake up mad, wondering what the hell was going on, and demand that I turn it all off immediately. I would look at him sleepily, and respond, "Why? It doesn't bother me." He would then get up completely irritated, turn everything off, and get back in the bed, in the hopes of having a peaceful sleep. I would then wait until he was almost to his happy sleepy place and turn everything on all over again. I would repeat this process regularly until I got bored, sleepy, or was satisfied that he at least felt a small measure of my pain.

I thought somehow, my frustration and complaining would make him see the error of his ways and encourage him to stay home with me and be a more loving and devoted husband. However it seemed like the more I complained, the more anxious he was to get away from me.

Imagine that. Our relationship was so passionate and volatile that I did not ever stop to think that my behavior was selfish; it just seemed like the most logical way to convey my feelings.

It was nearly a decade later when I finally got it. Something clicked in me as I was trying to find a way to escape my daughter's fifth grade dance. I called my best friend, and I asked her if she knew that I too was selfish. I said it as if it was a revelation, and she just laughed at me.

"Duh," she said, "how could you not know that?"

"I never saw it before." I told her. "I mean sure I thought I might be a little self-centered but that was all."

"Oh no!" she assured me. I was much more than that.

I asked for examples. I needed evidence, proof that I was indeed this thing that I had judged so harshly. She just continued to laugh in disbelief that I had only now realized it. It was a tough pill to swallow, and it took a little while to digest. Then the strangest thing happened, I began to embrace it.

I started to see all of the positive aspects and benefits of being selfish. I began viewing it as an underrated quality, and determined that the problem with me, as with most people, is not that we are too selfish, but that we are not selfish enough.

The other problem congruent to this one is the way in which we express this tendency. I realized that there were two possible expressions. One is love based; this is the good one that we don't see enough. The other is fear based, and this is the one that can be detrimental to relationships.

For all of those years I had been judging and behaving in a manner that expressed fear based selfishness. My actions were prompted by my fear of not having my needs met, and a fear that people were trying to take advantage of me. Everything I did was with the intention of offsetting, or counteracting, those possibilities. I wasn't putting myself first, but I was trying to force someone else to put me first.

It wasn't until I had a relationship where both he and I put our individual selves first that I understood the difference. In this relationship, when we told our truth and put ourselves first, the other person's needs were intrinsically met. By doing what he needed to do, he gave me room to do what I needed to do and vice versa. It was like synchronicity. The only thing that ever got in the way of this was the occasional bout of insecurity.

It occurred to me, sometime later, that if we are all universally connected, then this is the way the whole world should work. It should be that every person, by selfishly telling their truth, creates the opportunity for every connected person to live their truth as well. I wondered if this were so, what stood in the way of it. Then I remembered my own experience, and I immediately knew the answer.

Fear based selfishness, insecurity, and an unwillingness to live in accordance with personal truth; these are the things that stand in the way of it. These are the things that keep people from being with whom they are supposed to be, as well as the things that keep people together when they ought to move on.

Fear is a powerful force; it can either empower you, or imprison you. The antidote for fear is love. If you act always only out of love, there will be no room for fear in your life, and you will more frequently experience what can only be called kismet.

The problem we face in this country is that we are taught to put our kids first, and we burn ourselves out, trying to cater to their every need. Then in a moment of frustration, we lash out at them, sometimes with words and other times with actions.

If we were to shift that paradigm, and do as instructed by the flight attendant on an airplane, and put our own oxygen mask on first, we could breathe easy, while lovingly helping our kids instead of yelling at them to cooperate while we're gasping for air because we didn't stop to make sure our own needs were met.

For a lot of people this will be difficult to entertain. Caring for our kids is what we were built for. But let's face the reality. A crumbling building can't shelter anyone from the storm. As the parent, you are that building, or shelter, and you can't protect anyone if you're falling apart. It is more likely that pieces of you will land on, and injure, the very people you are trying to protect.

So let us realize that by giving ourselves what we need, we give our children permission to do the same as they grow up. After all, it's our example, not our words, which they will ultimately follow.

Action Plan: For Being More Selfish

1. Realize that if your needs are not being met you will not be in a position to meet anyone else's, at least not for very long.
2. Act out of love for yourself and treat other people according to the way in which you would show yourself love.
3. Show your children that you are deserving of love so that:

   a.) They will love you more.

   b.) They will love themselves more.

Do Not Make Idle Threats

Fear is a powerful motivator but only for as long as people are unwilling to face their fear. When dealing with children, we often use the fear of discipline to encourage positive behavior, but what happens when they obstinately refuse to respond favorably? What do you do when your child gets to the point where he or she is willing to find out what action is waiting on the other side of the words? One thing is for certain; if you do not do exactly what you said you would, you immediately lose all credibility.

I have found that in relationships, and child rearing, it is not a good idea to make threats you desire not to execute. That is not to say that you must never make threats, only that they must not be conclusive. All threats made should inspire fear, as well as be vague and intangible.

I learned this lesson first in my job as a school bus driver. As part of the minority to majority program, I shared a bus route with another driver. In the morning I would drive a bus load of African American kids from South Fulton County to North Fulton County, so that they could go to the predominantly white schools, in the hope of a better education, and she would drive them home in the afternoon.

One afternoon while she was driving, there was an incident with a student who was new to our bus. He started being very disruptive. She attempted to discipline him by making him sit in the front of the bus, but that only made things worse. He grew continuously more unruly to the point where she finally pulled the bus over on the highway. She radioed for assistance and informed her supervisor that the student was threatening her.

The word—threatening—triggered a violent and primal reaction in the child, whereby he began lashing out. The driver stood up and walked towards him with the intention of containing the situation, but he would not be contained. As she approached him, he immediately started assaulting her. He put her in a headlock and repeatedly punched her, alternately in the face and the stomach, until a couple of female students stepped in and attempted to stop him.

They grabbed his arm and held it so he could no longer hit her. Feeling the beating stop, the driver raised her head to regain her composure, and just as she did so, the student bit her just above the eye, ripping the skin from her face. Realizing what he had done, the student jumped off the bus and ran. It took several hours for anyone to find him.

Meanwhile, the bus driver was taken by ambulance to the hospital, and the rest of the students were transported home. The bus driver's wounds were treated, and she was stitched up and sent home. She ultimately suffered irreparable nerve damage as a result of the mistreatment of her wounds. Apparently, there are precautionary measures that should be taken when treating a human bite wound, which were omitted by the doctor that assisted her. As a result she had long-term vision and hearing impairments and was never able to return to work again.

Rumors of the incident spread trickling into various schools on both sides of the county. One day shortly thereafter, a child on my south county bus approached me, asking how I would respond if he assaulted me in that way. I told him he would not be able to do that to me. Again he asked what I would do. Recognizing that he was curious to the point of endangering one or both of us, I told him that if he even started walking up the aisle of the bus towards me, as if he was going to do something harmful, I would slam on the brakes, and he would go flying out the front window of the bus.

He did not believe me, and I knew I would never really try to endanger the life of this child, but I had already made the threat, and I couldn't back down now. I had to maintain my position and sell it convincingly enough to inspire so much fear in him that I would never have to see it through.

After several days of questioning me about how I would handle a situation, in which he attacked or assaulted me, he decided to test me. He got out of his seat and started walking up the aisle towards me. I could see in his eyes that his intention was not to harm me, but simply to prove that he could. My intention was to remove that notion as quickly as possible without actually causing him any injury.

As he walked towards me, I slammed on the brakes quickly and then released them, causing him to fly forward towards the window. I put my arm out to protect him from hitting the window, and then I told him to sit down before he killed himself.

He looked at me as if still uncertain whether or not I would actually harm him to protect myself. I picked up a large chock stick and told him without flinching, "Try me if you want to." Seeing the sincerity in my eyes he returned to his seat, and we never had to have that conversation again.

The point is, if you are going to make a threat, it has to be either something you are willing to follow through on, or at the very least, something that convinces the person you are threatening that you are sincere.

Years later I discovered that the same is true, whether it was the kids on the bus, my own children, or other adults I had relationships with.

With my personal kids, I learned that the more vague the threat the better. I just told them one day that if they did not listen to me when I told them the first time, they would not like the consequences at all if I had to tell them again. I would tell them something one time, and if they did not move immediately to respond to what I had said, I would start counting. I told them they better not let me get to three.

I didn't know any more than they did what exactly would happen if ever I got to three, but to ensure that we didn't find out, whenever I had to count, I would start with a very firm "TWO," and they would jump to attention and do whatever I had asked, or stop doing whatever it was they weren't supposed to be doing. My calling out two was like a warning shot, and my tone when I said it implied three was coming next, and I meant business. They rarely ever let me get to three.

There was one time where I believe they let me go to three, just out of curiosity, to see what would happen. I was a little irritated when that happened, because I knew that it was time to show and prove.

I did not like administering physical discipline, and my scare tactic had kept me from having to for some time. Now I had to make sure that it continued to work. I gave them the harshest age appropriate form of discipline I could, and then I made a big spectacle about how none if it would have happened if they had just done what I said before I got to three.

My daughter shouted out, "but that's not fair you always

skip one."

I told her, "One is the fact that you know you weren't supposed to be doing it in the first place. Two is your warning to stop, and three demands action."

My children are now teenagers, and they still rarely ever let me get to three. In fact when other people's children are around, they make sure those kids straighten up and act according to the rules of our home the minute I start counting.

Now regarding intimate relationships, it is more important than at any other time to not make idle threats. People, when confronted with a threat, have a tendency to want to see it through, as evidenced by the behavior of the children on the bus.

Adults, due to size, and life experiences, often lack the naturally embedded fear that children have. So, depending on their attachment to the relationship, they will either push you to follow through or stand down. Often, the fear of losing what they believe they have is enough to make them behave according to the desires of the person(s) they love. It is this fear that most people play on.

We occasionally hear people say if you don't behave in a certain way I am leaving. My advice is do not ever make a threat your not willing to implement because the likelihood is one day you will have to. If you know you have no desire to leave, do not suggest that you will for the sake of manipulation. Say what you mean and mean what you say, and remember, above all else, silence is your friend.

I am not saying that you should employ the silent treatment, which is another form of emotional blackmail. I am suggesting that if there is any doubt as to how you may act in a given situation, do not pretend to know. Simply keep your mouth shut until faced with that situation, and then in that moment, you have the full freedom to do whatever you desire, without being made to look like a liar. Even when you are in the midst of an action, do not make your intentions known. Just do what comes next until there is nothing more to do.

For example, let's say you go into a relationship telling your partner that you will never tolerate being hit by them; if they hit you even one time you are leaving. Then one day, in the midst of a heated discussion, they accidentally hit you. You both know it was an accident, but your threat had no contingency for accidents.

Now your options are, be a person of your word and leave a relationship you are not ready to end, or stay and risk getting hit intentionally next time, thus demonstrating that you are not going to do as you had previously stated; that you are in fact willing to stay and work through the occasional act of violence. Either way there is the potential for you to lose because you locked yourself into an action plan.

However, if you never say anything about what actions you will take in that situation, you have free reign to decide in the moment. Now if you are hit accidentally, you can either forgive, knowing full well that it was an accident, or you can leave for an undetermined period of time, to give the other person a chance to think about what he or she did, potentially come after you, and try to win you back. You are neither locked in by your pride, nor made to look like a liar.

When I was in Bequia one year, I found myself in a situation where I fell in love with a man who was torn between the woman he was already dating and me. There was one particular occasion where she was supposed to be coming to town, and I pleaded for him to not allow it. He told me he would take care of it; he would tell her not to come.

I was relieved until his friends came in the restaurant, prodding and chiding me about her impending arrival. Suddenly my pride kicked in, and for some reason, I either did not believe him, or I was upset that I had to plead my case to get him to make what should have been an obvious decision.

In a moment of strength, I told myself that I did not need him, and I deserved more than to compete with some other girl for the affection of a man. I sent him a text message telling him he should tell the girl to come. I did not feel like I should have to compete for his attention, and I was taking myself out of the game. The moment I sent that text, I regretted it. I tried to call and undo it, but the words were already out, and he refused to answer the phone after reading them. I was distraught over my haste to make my pride known, and that entire night I could not sleep.

The next day I called again, and finally he answered. I asked him if the girl had come to town, and he told me she had. "Why did you do that?" I asked him.

He replied simply "What did your text say?"

"Well you know I didn't mean it." I told him.

To which he replied, "I don't know what you meant, I know what you said."

I thought to myself, "That was just an excuse for you to do what you were going to do anyway." What I learned though was to not say things I wasn't sure I meant, and especially, to not make idle threats that might have consequences I may not want to live with.

I learned a lot about silence that year while dealing with this man of few words. When I acted in a way he did not care for, there was no argument. He showed me with his actions how it felt by making me feel it for myself. This method insured that those acts would not be thoughtlessly repeated. Additionally, when I made threats he gave me the opportunity to follow through, which I rarely wanted to do.

I loved him way too much to just walk away, so instead I kept my words to a minimum and learned how to let my actions speak for me. It's like the saying goes, actions speak louder than words. Most threats have to be constantly repeated; an action only has to be done one time.

Warning: Be careful too about which actions you take knowing that for every action there is an equal and opposite reaction. Be cautious, and calculated, and don't do anything that may have consequences you will have difficulty living with.

Action Plan: For Not Making Threats

1. Say what you mean and mean what you say.
2. If you're unsure what you mean, give yourself some wriggle room.
3. Employ silence and vagueness; they are your allies.
4. If you do make a threat and you are called on it, follow through. This is very important as it affects the level of respect and treatment you get from that person from that point on.

If You Lock the Dog in the Room The Whole House Will Stink

Many very wise people have opted to parent pets instead of children; they were my inspiration here. This is my reminder to them to be careful with whom you leave your pets, because some people won't love them the way you do. Additionally this chapter is a metaphor for life. Hiding your problems will not make them go away. It will only cause them to grow larger and more damaging.

We as people have a tendency to take an ostrich approach to life and bury our head in the sand believing that if we can't see the issues they don't exist. Even worse we believe we are smarter than average and therefore capable of "pulling the wool over the eyes" of others and thereby get away with doing something we perhaps ought not to have done.

I, for one, am guilty, on occasion, of thinking I am going to get away with something, and life has proven to me over and over again that no matter how resourceful I am, I will suffer the consequences of my actions, one way or another, even when I think I am not doing any harm.

Ralph Waldo Emerson opened my eyes to this through his essay entitled *Compensation,* in which he clearly details this often-disregarded universal law. Though I know I am by no means doing the essay justice by what I am here writing, I still wish to share with you what I got from it.

No matter what we do in life, or what another does, it is impossible to get away with anything. We will either be hunted by the law, or haunted by our conscience, and it is impossible to tell from the outside looking in which experience is worse. For the law of compensation works hand in hand with another law, which states: it is impossible to injure another person without also causing yourself injury. Likewise it is impossible help another person without also helping yourself. So know, just as sure as the world is round, what goes around comes around.

I once made the mistake of thinking that this law only applied to our relationships with people. It took me only three days to learn that pets are people too.

You see, I am not a pet person. I don't own any pets, primarily because I do not want to be responsible for anything that can't ask for or prepare its own food. I do love animals but mostly from a distance. I like to think that we have a healthy respect for each other, and so long as they stay out of my way, I stay out of theirs. I believe we all fare better that way.

Interestingly, all of my friends have pets. I have one who had so many cats living in her house at one time; I developed an allergy to cats simply from going to visit her. Were it not for her extremely high sex drive, I would have worried that she were destined to be a spinster.

I have another who had a dog that was too big for her to handle. He didn't start out that way of course, but as he grew in size, he grew out of control, and her docile temperament was no match for her rambunctious puppy. She ultimately ended up locking him in the spare room of the house until her husband could get around to taking him out. As it turned out, it was her husband she should have been locking in the room. So the lesson here was; had my friend's husband not been in the streets doing his own dirt, his house would not have smelled like his dog when he finally did arrive.

At least that was his lesson as I saw it. The other lesson for me in all this was to be careful when you laugh at, and judge your friends because you are merely dooming yourself to suffer the same experience. This lesson I didn't learn fully until a decade later.

I allowed my cousin and her family to move in with me because she didn't want to move back in with her parents. It was my cousin, her two daughters, their two pet ferrets, and her dog. I was aware of my reasons for not wanting pets, but I did not know how strong my resistance to them was until one weekend she left me alone in the house with her dog.

Originally, my daughter had volunteered to walk the dog, and feed it, and such, but she ended up going away for the weekend, and that left me as the sole custodian of the dog. I was not comfortable with that responsibility even for a few days.

The dog was a small well-mannered lapdog that caused no trouble at all, but I was emotionally bankrupt at the time and mentally incapable of small acts of humanity.

So like my wonderful friend that I had judged—perhaps a bit harshly—I took the dog and locked it in the bathroom. It was the location in which I deemed it would make the least mess and where the smell could be removed with the greatest ease. Thinking myself intelligent enough to learn from my friend's mistake, I opted to not put the dog in a room with carpet. And while it was true that I had learned that lesson, there was a greater one waiting for me around the corner.

It was the one that made me aware that it is impossible to hurt, or imprison another living being without also doing the same to yourself. For the entire time I had the dog locked in the bathroom, I had myself locked in the bedroom. It was like some weird psychosomatic bond or something, but to the extent that I made that dog uncomfortable, I did the same to myself. After three days of depressing solitude, I let us both out, and I have since developed a greater respect for life, and the connection we all share.

The point, in case you missed it, is this. Be aware of how

you treat, and what you do to others, because it always comes right back around on you. The Bible says you reap what you sow. The golden rule says due unto others, as you would have them do unto you. The reason for this is that everything you do to or for another, you do to or for yourself as well. At some point in the long run, or the short run, you will be given the opportunity to experience the very same treatment you have shown to another person or pet.

Action Plan: For Proper Treatment

1. Put yourself in their shoes. How would you honestly like to be treated? Do that for them.
2. Realize that our pets' needs are similar to our own, and because we've taken them from their element and rendered them helpless, we have assumed full responsibility for them.
3. Remember if you enslave them you will become a slave to them. If you love them you will be loved by them.
4. Very simply put you get what you give.

If You're Going to Lie, Lie About the Future

Everybody lies, the truth shall set you free, everything done in the dark comes to light et cetera, et cetera. Clichés abound when it comes to lying, but the consensus seems to be that lying is bad, and everybody does it.

That has been the premise for more than one popular television show, but does that make it true? If it is true, what does that say about us? Is there honestly anything wrong with lying?

Some who consider themselves honest and truthful can be harsh critics of the more obvious liar, but does this mean that they are not ever dishonest? The reality is that the propensity for lying is as indelibly ingrained on our psyche as the desire for truth. In each and every one of us, there is a trigger which when activated will cause us to fabricate for one reason or another. We all have different triggers and different perspectives on what is acceptable.

Some people have an impulse to lie like a hair trigger and will omit, deny, or disguise any truth that makes them

136

uncomfortable to tell. Others will admit to things, only after scrupulous goading, and/or proof that they have been found out. Some are forthright about all the big things and don't believe the little things they lie about such as those that pertain to their emotional, mental, or physical state should even count as lies. Still, there are those who lie to protect and spare others discomfort and therefore feel justified in the belief that they have done a good deed.

As with every other crime, there are about a hundred different motives for every method and an endless number of reasons for the criminal offense. That's not to imply that a lie is a crime; only that it is often treated like one.

When I was in my late teens, I found myself in a situation where I felt backed into a corner. I had asked my grandparents, with whom I lived, for permission to spend the night at a friend's house. I left home fully intending to do just that. Unfortunately, as this was before the prevalence of cell phones, I found myself unable to get in contact with my friend.

As I was already out with other friends, I decided to just continue what I was doing and enjoy myself before returning home. As luck would have it, I got home extremely late and had forgotten my house key. This had become a habit with which my grandmother had grown extremely frustrated. She told me if I forgot my key again, I needed to stay with whomever I was with because she didn't want me waking her up in the middle of the night to answer the door. Well, I did exactly as I was instructed.

I went home early the next morning hoping to sneak in unnoticed, but the house was abuzz. Everyone was awake and seemed to be waiting on me. When I walked in, my grandmother asked me, "How was Tameka's house?" To which I replied, "It was fine I suppose." I was trying to be clever with my words so as not to feel like I was lying. I should have known by the way she was asking that she was trying to trap me, but instead I fell right in.

She said she knew I didn't go to Tameka's, and she was going to report me to the older men of the congregation so they could counsel me on lying. I was glad to have to deal with them and not her. Her disapproval was by far more unbearable then anything they could possibly say to me.

When they arrived, we spoke for hours on the topic of lying. They asked me what I thought about it, and if I felt like I was wrong for doing it. Then they said the thing that I felt let me off the hook. They said, "No one lie is better or worse then any other lie." That opened the door for me to the turn the tables on them.

I told one of them "If that is true sir, then my misrepresenting where I was last night is no worse then you telling me you're feeling fine when you're suffering from back aches and knee pain."

The elder I was speaking to replied, "That is kind of true, but nobody wants to hear about all the pain I am in."

"Then they shouldn't ask you how you are doing," I continued. "Maybe if you tell them the truth enough times, they will stop asking, or maybe they will show genuine concern and offer you the help you need. If a lie is a lie and no one is better then any other one, then we all lie on a daily basis. So while I appreciate your effort and concern I don't really believe that you can justify sitting here counseling me on the very same thing you do regularly."

They tried to get a few more points in before concluding the meeting, but ultimately decided that I was ornery and reluctant to heed counsel. I, of course, disagreed opting instead to believe myself to be a person who was open to any wisdom or truth presented logically, which I could find application for in my life.

I am not in any way an advocate of lying. In fact, I stand staunchly against it. In most cases it causes more problems than it solves and hurts more people than it helps. There is actually nothing I hate more than being lied to.

Some years later when I got married, my husband cheated on me. Though I had previously believed that was something I could never tolerate, I decided in that moment I could forgive him and accept it, provided he told me the truth about the situation.

Fearing the consequences of his honesty more than his actions, he chose to continue lying, and I chose to divorce him. I was unwilling to spend my life living with a liar. Ironically, a year or two later when our daughter started speaking in complete and coherent sentences, I discovered that she was inherently predisposed toward fabrication.

I think she inherited it from her father or something. If that girl got the slightest indication that she was in trouble, she had a lie ready on her lips.

There was one occasion where she threw a shoe at her brother and hit him with it. He started crying and told me what happened. When I questioned her, she staunchly denied it. I had to trick her into telling me the truth, and then I disciplined her, not for throwing the shoe, but for lying.

Over the years this behavior became a pattern, so in an effort to break it, I sat her down, and explained to her the potential consequences of lying. I told her that if she lied to me, I would be unable to trust her. In the event she was actually accused of something she didn't do, I wouldn't know to believe or defend her because of the reputation she had created for herself. I explained to her that, more than anything, I wanted to protect her from harm, but she made it hard for me to do that by lying to me and putting me in a position where I could not trust anything she said to be true. I told her, I would rather her tell me nothing at all, than look me in my face and lie to me.

Why on earth did I say that? It took me six years after that to realize that she had adopted silence as a means of communication. No matter how much she wanted to, she could not bring herself to admit wrongdoing. Whenever questioned she would look at me with guilty eyes, and a closed mouth, and I would know the truth she refused to speak. I began to wonder what this thing was that so compelled one of my children to lie, and the other to speak truth, even if it meant he was going to be harshly disciplined.

I detested lying so greatly that on the rare occasions I did it, I would generally go back and admit the truth within a matter of hours, no more than a day or so. That being said, there is one area of life where I do feel it is ok to lie, if you want to call it that, but before I get to that I would like to explore why we should not lie.

The problem with lies is in what we lie about and why we lie in the first place. Most people lie about their past or about things that have already occurred in the mind, if not also with the body. However, I find misrepresenting the past to be counterintuitive because there is undoubtedly some evidence that the truth will at the most inconvenient time surface and ruin your credibility, and your character. As a result, you will lose the respect of the people whose opinions you value and your integrity.

There exists, it seems in almost every person, a subconscious belief that they are above the laws of the universe where lying is concerned. Everything done in the dark will come to light is a universal law, and yet we see droves of people daily convincing themselves that their "secret" behaviors and actions will never be found out.

Some hide the truth as a way to protect themselves from unfavorable consequences, while others tell themselves they are protecting their loved ones from pain. There is another group that lies for the purpose of fitting in, while a very few do it just to stand out. The reason that this is so ineffective is that one, we are all connected, and that cannot be broken by a desire to stand out or fit in. Two, all actions are eventually exposed, and the consequences, as well as the pain caused, are much greater when they are only revealed by the unveiling of a misrepresentation of the facts.

The greatest benefit of truth as I see it is longevity. Relationships recover faster when there's honesty. Not that we won't still make mistakes that may be painful for some to accept, but the admittance of such mistakes gives the relationship a leg to stand on—a foundation based on truth, which breeds trust and respect.

Outside of personal relationships, we can see the same rules apply to people's careers. When you hear a performer pour their personal truth into a performance, it creates an opportunity for you to connect with them at the level of the soul. The artists that stay relevant are the ones that rip themselves open, and let us see who they truly are for better or for worse. The people who just try to capitalize off of the fads of the time and their talent may have limited success, but the minute we see the slightest hint of deceit, their careers end in the same flash of light they began.

One of the longest running inside jokes is the one about truth in comedy. Most people think comedy is about telling jokes, but the most successful comedians are the ones who tell their truth. There is a similar consensus regarding truth in advertising. If you look closely enough, you will see that this rule applies to every major position in every field in every industry.

Granted, there are a great many people, who find success in spinning the truth, and there are some who would say that spin is the same as lying, but I disagree. Life has taught me that though it is extremely important to tell the truth, there are a lot of people who still do not want to hear it. Sometimes spinning it, or wording it ambiguously, helps those people to remain safe in the bubble of ignorance that affords them the level of comfort they most desire for their life.

The reason I see nothing wrong with this is because I am all too aware of how blissful ignorance can be. There were a great many days that I wished I could go back to my own previous state of bliss. Yes knowledge is power, but power can be down right exhausting. In those moments, blissful ignorance can seem like a peaceful place to rest. However, I don't recommend resting in ignorance too long because information is constantly changing, and you don't want to get left behind.

The bottom line is any lie that history can prove untrue is not beneficial. However lies about the future can be. Because the future has not happened yet, every statement made regarding it is untrue. The beauty of this type of lie is the opportunity it affords us to realize it, and make it true. The mere act of telling such a lie initiates an internal striving for verity.

I am not sure you can even call it lying, because the reality is that anything you say about your future is a fabrication, until it isn't anymore. The mistake that we often make though is we tell ourselves negative things about what our future holds, and we feel dishonest if we say something positive.

Whether negative or positive, a statement made about the future is neither true nor untrue, until it is backed up by action proving, or disproving it. So, if you are going to make a statement about your future, make it a positive one, and then prove it to be true through your actions.

Likewise, if you make a statement about your past make it an honest one, and deal with whatever consequences may follow knowing that they will be far less severe if you deal with them upfront. Remember, the truth is going to come out eventually. You may as well be the one to tell it. Also keep in mind, truth cannot go unrecognized, and universal laws cannot be broken. In a world that is always evolving, the one constant is truth. So use your true desires to create your real future.

Action Plan: For Lying

1. Do not make any statement that will diminish your integrity. When it comes to integrity, the cold hard truth elicits a better response than a little white lie.
2. When speaking about the future, say positive things even if your present feels bleak and there is no hope on the horizon.
3. Strive to keep your word. It will lead to the best manifestation of your life.

Use Your Words

When I was nine years old, my mother's boyfriend touched me inappropriately. He would sit next to me, put his hand under my seated position, and wriggle his fingers around in what I can only assume was an attempt to stimulate me. It made me feel so uncomfortable, I would move. He in turn moved closer and continued to touch me until I got up and walked out of the room. As I departed I told him I was going to tell my mother, to which he replied, "If you tell on me I will tell on you." I was not sure what he was going to tell on me because I had not done anything. Still, the threat worked.

It instilled just enough fear in me to get me to keep my mouth shut. He apparently took my silence as permission to continue molesting me, and every time I found myself in a room alone with him, he would find some kind of way to slide his hand in the direction of my private parts and wriggle his fingers around. It made me feel uncomfortable to move freely in my home. As a result, I would either stay in my own room, which he didn't enter, or only go in the rooms my mother was

146

in. If she left the room, I had to leave as well, or he was coming for me.

After a few weeks of this I told my mother what was going on, to which she said, "Okay." I thought okay meant she was going to handle it by doing something to this man to get him back for what he was doing to me. A few weeks later she broke up with him. For years I thought they had broken up because of what I told her. I later learned she did not even recall me telling her such a thing. She had ended the relationship with that man because he was stealing from her. I would have been happy to go my whole life never knowing that.

At the age of ten my brothers would invite their friends into our home when my mother was away and command them to attack me, at which time they would try to feel me up while I rolled my self in a ball and screamed for them to stop. This game was apparently fun for them—not so much for me.

At eleven my cousin molested me. He was actually the first person to ever make direct physical contact with my vagina. The minute his finger entered my body I got up and ran to the door threatening to tell my father, who was in the other room getting high with my aunt. Again I was silenced by the threat of him telling on me. For what reason, I was still unsure, but again, the threat worked.

Five years later when I saw my cousin again, I confronted him about what he had done to me. He apologized for it, and I forgave him. Two weeks later he raped me in my sleep. I have yet to forgive him for that one. That time I told my mother, who told my aunt, who insisted we were going to do something about it. Nothing was ever done about it. It was swept under the rug right along with my self-esteem and boundaries.

Over the years that followed, I suffered through several more acts of molestation and rape by various family members, and each time, I handled the situation pretty much the same way I had been handling it since I was nine. I walked away from the perpetrator, and at some point told my mother.

My mother in many of these cases actually confronted the perpetrators, and they admitted to what they had done to me. Still, I was being silently blamed for bringing these issues into the family. I was so confused; I had no idea what I had done wrong, nor what I should have done differently.

Now, I am the proud parent of an eleven-year-old girl who is excited about the development of her breasts. My horror grows proportionately to her cup size because I know she will soon be faced with some uncomfortable and compromising situations, and I may not always be there to protect her. So I am trying to figure out what I can tell her that will help her to not have to go through what I went through.

I found myself feeling lost, because I could not teach my child what I didn't know. If I had known how to prevent men from making unwanted sexual advances towards me, I would have done that along time ago. I looked to her father to do it, but he seems to think I am better equipped to handle the situation, as I am known for being good with words. The irony is that I am half way through my thirties, and I have only just learned that it is words, or the lack there of, that have gotten me into as much trouble as they have gotten me out of.

This particular piece of information that I am about to share with you is so new to me that I have not as yet even had the chance to try it out. For some of you this is going to sound very obvious; like common sense. Others like me will feel like a light bulb just went on in their head as they grasp hold of this enlightening new concept.

I received this information during an argument with my cousin, to whom I am so grateful to for staying in the argument with me, until I finally got it. She was upset with me because she felt like I was misrepresenting myself and leading her friend to believe that I had an interest in having sex with him. I told her in no uncertain terms that I at no point had any intentions of being in any way intimate with him. To which she retorted, "That was not how it looked to me or any of the other people in our party."

"I have a strong sexual presence," I said "People often get the impression that I am interested in them in that way when I am not. I can't control that."

"Yes you can." she said, "You can choose to not entertain them when they come onto you."

"I was not entertaining him," I told her. "I was trying to be polite, but he kept coming at me cock first like his only interest was in having sex, so every time he came at me disrespectfully, I just walked away. I did not want to create a negative or uncomfortable situation, given that we were riding in his car, so I just bided my time, and avoided him until it was time to leave."

She then said the most profound thing. She said, "You were giving him mixed messages, you should have simply told him that you had no interest in having sex with him, and that you did not appreciate him talking to you like that."

The thing was, in this particular case, I had told him that I did not have intentions of having sex with him, but apparently I was not firm enough in my position. I led him to believe that there was a possibility I would reconsider my decision given enough gentle persuasion. I knew, without a doubt, that I was not going to be convinced of anything along those lines, but apparently I did not convey that.

The point is, when I explained to her that my way of handling it was to walk away, and she retorted that I should have declared my intentions or lack thereof, three decades of improperly handled interactions came flooding into my head, and then it clicked. I was being reactive, when I should have been proactive. I should have loudly, and firmly said to the man when I was nine, stop it; I do not like that, instead of just walking away.

When my cousin ignored my eleven-year-old pleas to stop because I didn't like what he was doing, I should have screamed. There is an accepted protocol of behavior that when followed helps to keep the victim from being blamed for the act of molestation or rape, but I was not made aware of it until it was too late. I am making my daughter aware of it now in the hopes that she will never have to endure the things I have been through. And I am writing this with the hopes that it will benefit you and yours as well.

I am the product of generations of women who were raped or molested by men and silenced by the women in their own family. It is my goal to not just break the cycle but to educate us on the simple things, which seem like common sense that so many of us don't know. At nine, when my boundaries were crossed, and my voice was silenced, I developed a pattern of behavior that has worked against me my entire life. At thirty-six, I am changing it and doing everything in my power to help others like me.

So here is the protocol. When a man approaches you in a way that is inappropriate, or disrespectful, use your words firmly and directly to shut him down the first time. If you laugh, giggle, or play coy, he perceives that as interest, and you have in that very moment devalued yourself because now he thinks you're easy, and with a little persuasion he can have his way with you. If you allow this to continue, and persuasion does not seem to be working, he may resort to force.

If a man attempts to force himself on you, **SCREAM** as loud as you can, and try to get away from him. Fighting back is not enough. You have to scream. Some men see fighting as foreplay. They will assume that you are just playing hard to get. A loud shrill sincere scream is unmistakable. If there was a misunderstanding that got you in this position, screaming will effectively clear it up.

If a man succeeds in forcing himself on you, in spite of you firmly telling him you are not interested and screaming, report it right away. Try to remember everything you can about this person and look for identifying marks. This will help in getting these individuals off of the street so that another woman will not have to endure what you have been through.

If you have already been the victim of rape or molestation, and you did not follow this protocol, it is still not your fault. You did what you knew to do at the time, and that is something to be proud of. All you can do is what you know to do, and when you know better you do better. It took me three decades to learn better and make the connection that a pattern of behavior I adopted as an innocent child has been a controlling force in my life, and standing in the way of my progress.

I thought back to all of the potential opportunities I missed, because I walked away when whatever man I happened to be dealing with said something inappropriate, instead of just shutting down that line of conversation, and reasserting my purpose for being there. It makes me sad to know there was something so simple I could have done but happy that I now know and can share it with my daughter.

Because of the way I look, and the energy I project, I am faced with sexual advances and harassment all the time. I accepted it as normal, but wondered why this did not seem to happen to every other woman. I actually believed there was something wrong with the women it did not happen to. I thought they were prudes who were oversensitive to words.

The truth was, they had standards, and boundaries, and the awareness that the more open you are to those words in casual conversation, the more it shapes and changes the way men see, and value you to the point where they declare you worthless, and take advantage of you in such a manner that they would not tolerate happening to their own mother or sister.

For more insight on how you as a woman should expect to be treated by a man, I highly recommend Steve Harvey's book, *Act Like a Lady Think Like Man*, and please, please, please let your daughter know it is okay to say firmly and definitively "I am not interested in you. I have no intentions of being in any way intimate with you. I am sorry if I misled you, or you misinterpreted something I said or did, but I do not want to be with you."

Even if you desire to flirt but wish it not to go any further, it is ok to say that, and make it clear. Say, "I really enjoy flirting with you, but I have no desire to take it any further than a friendly flirtation." The sooner you make clear your desires and intentions, or the lack thereof, the better chance you have of safe guarding yourself against unwanted advances.

Also a good rule of thumb, if you are uncertain as to how far you are willing to go with a particular individual, is to say no first. It is much easier to say yes later. If you tell him up front that you have no intentions towards sex or intimacy, and as the night progresses you decide you do, it will be better for both of you. You will feel better knowing that you have removed the expectation from the equation, and he will feel better believing that he won you over than he would if he felt like you led him on.

Action Plan: For Using Your Words

1. Be clear and be direct in asserting your intentions.
2. Follow the protocol. Say No, or I'm not interested, scream run if you can. If it happens against your will, press charges.
3. If you have already been the victim of mistreatment remember it is not your fault and forgive yourself.
4. Teach others how to protect themselves as well. Pass it on, pay it forward, whatever it takes to break the cycle, do it.

Part 4

Obvious Truths About Work

Your work is going to fill a large part of your life, and the only way to be truly satisfied is to do what you believe is great work. And the only way to do great work is to love what you do. If you haven't found it yet, keep looking. Don't settle."
— *Steve Jobs*

We Love What We Serve

As humans we are hard wired to love that to which we render service. I state this hypothesis as proof not only that we were created by a God or higher power, but as a testament to His brilliance. To some this may seem counterintuitive, as popular wisdom would lead us to believe that we love first, and then render service to that which we love, but I have come to understand that the reverse is true.

It occurred to me when I reflected back on the beauty of child bearing. This is the basis for all human connection and the proof of my hypothesis. I am a mother of two, and at the time that I was carrying my first child, pregnancy felt like an attack had been launched on my body. I was surrounded by people basking in the joy of the miracle growing inside of me. Meanwhile, I was deeply aware of the miracle that was required for me to permit such a happenstance.

It all begins with an act of pleasure. The moment attraction is felt our bodies heat up. The closer we get proximally to the object of our attraction, our bodies respond and react to our apparent desires, sending out all sorts of signals that stimulate, and enlarge our sexual organs. Unable to fight the urge, we give in to the sensations and have intercourse. When done properly, intercourse climaxes into a combustible explosion, whereby we release our life force into each other. It is an uncontrollable biological function, and any attempt to hold back from allowing this process to occur results in pain, the likes of which no man wishes to endure.

When our life forces combine, at the right time, with the right thrust and energy, a cell begins to multiply where an egg once lived, and we as women give our entire bodies over to the service of this cell. We have little control over it and are not given many options. Our service to this being starts from within.

For forty weeks, we feed, grow, and nurture what we call our baby. We provide it a safe place to develop and make sure it gets all the nutrients required for its development. We touch it, rub it, and talk to it. We sleep more than normal, so that our body can give its energy to the person within, and it is usually a very demanding little person. He or she tells us when and what to eat, when to sleep, pee, and cry. When the baby has sufficiently developed to live outside of us, it signals our body to push it out, with no regard to the damage it did to our bodies while it was in there and no apology for the scars it leaves on the way out.

The strange thing is, as women, we don't even care (that

much). The more energy we put into serving that baby while it's inside of us, the more we grow to love it, but the service doesn't end when the baby comes out. It can be said that birth was just the beginning.

After birth, the real work begins. Caring for that child becomes our full-time job, and we happily devote every waking (and sleeping) moment to the care of our newborn. We use our bodies to feed them, and once they process the food, and put it back out, we rush to clean up the mess. We hold, coddle, and talk to them in our softest sweetest baby voice, and we rock them in our arms until they fall asleep. If they cry while we sleep, we wake to tend to their needs, be it for food, changing, or gas, which we politely call colic.

We jump up alarmed every time they cry and even more so if they go too long without crying. Every mother knows the silence that is scarier than the crying and the gasp that comes after injury but prior to outburst. By the length of the gasp, we can tell the extent of injury our child has suffered and how long the tears will flow.

We watch in awe as they grow and try to capture, and record every detail of their development, in our memory, on film, and or video. We not only want to make sure that we don't miss anything, we want to be able to go back, and look on again with fondness, at the life to which we rendered the greatest service.

The irony is that the greater the amount of service you

render to this person that grew inside of you, the greater the amount of love you grow to have for it. One would think it would be the other way around; that the more you had to do for the child the more you would resent it. However, resentment only surfaces when you are not there for the baby, and it is usually a side effect of guilt.

Looking at anyone who has had a difficult pregnancy can provide evidence of this. When a woman actually has to work or rest excessively to get her baby here safely, it creates a different, and dare I say stronger, bond. The same is true of people with sickly children who, even as they grow, they have to continue to do everything for them, or live in constant fear that their life may be taken away. These people usually seem to have a greater sense of love and protectiveness over their children.

Do not misunderstand me; there are some exceptions. As I said, we love what we serve, but only to the degree that we feel fulfilled or satisfied, by the identity that the acts of service provide us. If on the other hand we feel like what we serve is unfulfilling, or hindering us in some way from our perceived purpose, we grow to hate what we serve.

This can be seen not only with regard to mothering children, but also in professions where some people love their job, while others who do the exact same thing hate it. Again, the perceived knowledge regarding this runs counter to what I am saying because most people will tell you, "do what you love, and you will never work a day in your life." However, again I say that service comes first. The truth is, you don't know what you love until you do something, and often, in order to find what you love, you have to do many things first.

What I suggest in this regard is do many things until you find one that resonates with you internally and leads you to believe it could be something to which you would not mind devoting a great deal of your time, with little benefit other than the act of the service itself. Then render as much service as you can to this thing until you know it fully. At this point, others will consider you a professional regarding this activity or subject, and they will pay you handsomely for your knowledge and ability regarding the thing you served so much you grew to love it.

Due to societal branding men are more inclined to live their lives in this way than women, for men are taught early on that they have to work for what they want. They grow up believing they have to render service to achieve the object of their desire.

With regard to employment, they are told they have to work their way to the top. When they find the company or career where they wish to make it to the top, they make no qualms about the process.

With regard to women, men are taught not to value the ones that make it too easy. They are told that easy women serve the purpose of giving them pleasure, while they wait, and look for the one who will make them work for it. In many cases, women sabotage themselves by giving too much of themselves too soon. Men need to be needed.

Men have a need to serve women, and when he feels appreciated by the woman he is serving, his love for her will grow. It begins with attraction, and he will let her know if he is attracted to her, but if she doesn't give him the opportunity to pursue her and render service to her, his focus will change regarding her, and he will move on to find a woman who needs him and allows him to serve her.

Often a woman may wonder why the man to whom she devotes all of her time, attention, resources, and love will leave her for a woman who doesn't give nearly as much. The answer is in the question. It is because she doesn't give nearly as much. In a man's mind, the woman who starts off giving less has more to give and has likely given less away to other men. He thinks because she is holding back she recognizes her value, and if she knows her worth then he will honor whatever value or price she gives herself. It's not logical. It is just the way men think.

Not only that, but a woman who knows her value will automatically deter all of the wrong men because they will know instinctively that she is out of their league, or budget, or what ever you want to call it. The bottom line is, when you assign yourself a greater value, and you don't settle for less you will attract what you're worth, and the great part is, you decide what you're worth.

Now here is where it gets tricky. Just as giving services makes us feel love for a person or thing, receiving service makes us feel loved by a person, or group, or anything capable of love.

Therefore, if you have a man in your life that you wish to hold onto, it is important to not serve him until you know that he loves you. According to Steve Harvey in his book *Act Like A Lady Think Like A Man,* you will know a man loves you when he demonstrates *"The Three P's"* and they are, "proclaim, protect, and provide." If a man isn't willing to tell you and others that he loves you, protect you from harm, and provide for your needs, do not assume he loves you no matter what he says in the heat of the moment.

If you don't care where the relationship goes, then by all means do what feels right in the moment, so long as it falls in line with your personal moral code, but if you want something lasting, it is important to follow the rules of longevity and let the man see your worth, through your ability to let him serve you, before you show him how willing you are to serve him back.

Action Plan: For Serving Your Interest

1. Explore all of your interests until you find the one you are willing to do for free, and often.
2. Devote as much energy as you can to the service of that thing.
3. Acknowledge regularly all of the things you like, love, or enjoy about it.
4. With regard to friends, and family recognize the effect of service on your relationships.

Crazy or Genuis: What's the Difference?

It amazes me actually the way people perceive genius. For years, I have said that the only difference between crazy and genius is proof. My logic was that historically, every genius we have popularized was thought to be mad until the point at which they were able to prove their theories.

Once the proof was there, then people touted them as genius. At least this is true in the fields of science and math. However in artistic genres like language, art, and music, geniuses are not called crazy until long after their masterpiece or work of genius is created.

This leads me to believe that the only difference between the people we initially call genius and the people we ultimately call crazy is the way in which they channel their pain.

Crazy people devoid of genius turn their pain inward. They live in their minds and torture themselves for all to see and none to help. They go to a place in their head, where they are unreachable, because that is the only place they feel safe, and we, instead of trying to make it safe for them out here,

164

give them medication, so that we can better tolerate their pain.

It does not make the pain go away; it simply makes us more comfortable in their presence. The nature of normal people is very much self-absorbed with a greater interest in the appearance of things than in the reality of things. Crazy people don't care how things appear. They don't have the mental space for it. There is always so much going on inside of their head demanding their attention; they lose sight of what is going on outside of it.

Geniuses, on the other hand, both creative and scientific, turn their pain outward. They deflect it onto their work so that through their work we see the madness in them. For them the process of the work itself is so cathartic, it allows them to function semi-normally in society.

In the cases of both creative and scientific genius, the process begins with a love or a passion for something the person feels good about, competent at, or compelled to do. This thing allows them to either escape reality, or makes it easier to face it. Whether they will face reality or escape it depends on where they are in working through their demons, but the processes for both are very similar. Once you discover what it is you have a love for then you work on that thing, regularly and consistently.

This is where it gets a little confusing because for some, creativity comes in fits and spurts and is therefore not something that can be tapped into at will, but in this case, one needs only to give in to the process. When the spurt comes, you go for it full-fledged and do not stop until it goes.

Others learn to devote several hours of each day to the art, and the level of productivity is what comes in spurts. Some days will feel as though nothing was accomplished, and other days will produce works of art.

On both days they will be thankful for the process because it has helped to control the well of emotion building up inside of them and causing an aggravating moody disposition. At the least there is the awareness that some good was done just by putting forth the effort.

So now, we have love or passion, and a consistent pattern of performing, but we are still lacking in material. There are tons of thoughts passing through our heads all day everyday, so how do we know which ones to pull out and which to leave in there?

The truth is we don't, and that is why vulnerability is so important. It alerts us to where our passions lie, leaving us no choice but to focus on its cause. It makes us stop for a moment, tap in, and ask ourselves what is the origin of this feeling. As we explore the source of the vulnerability, we find ourselves overwhelmed with emotion.

We find ourselves facing past issues we believed to be resolved. Only there was no resolution, it was just suppression masquerading as personal growth. The real problem was lurking in the shadows, waiting for the opportunity to come out and be rectified. Wasn't that nice of emotion to sit back and allow you to function with seeming normalcy, until you reached a point where you felt safe enough to deal with it?

I know what you're thinking. You're thinking that safe is not the word you would use to describe anything related to vulnerability, and therein lies the irony.
Vulnerability is an emotion that can only be felt when a certain level of safeness is present.

In the heat of battle, or the heat of any moment for that matter, we do not allow ourselves the luxury of being vulnerable. We are too busy fighting for our lives and, in some cases, our livelihood. We operate on pure adrenaline, mentally and physically, using and channeling all of our resources toward staying alive. We do not feel any pain, only occasional anger, or rage, and we use that to further feed the adrenaline. For the most part we are completely numb.

We turn our bodies off and only release the components necessary for survival. We interact with people from a place of detached distance, because we don't know for sure who our enemies are. We have often been so violated, mutilated, or taken advantage of; we fear the same fate belies us in every person we meet. Guarded, we walk through life like soldiers through a war zone, waiting for God or somebody to call a cease-fire.

Sometimes we may cry, but those are not the tears of a vulnerable person. They are the tears of a person who is pissed off and overwhelmed at having been in a situation that calls for a life devoid of true feeling, for periods longer than that person wishes to endure. Those tears are a mere release of pent up frustration and resentment for being in a situation that is less than pleasant.

It is only when we are once again made to feel that vulnerability can enter the picture, but it doesn't come just because we want it to. It waits until the feelings are pleasurable, until you are within reach of happiness, and then like a floodgate, it comes crashing down, threatening to take it all away. This is when the true battle begins; the battle within us to go after what we want or allow vulnerability to deter us with its counterpart, insecurity.

If they get together and tag-team you, watch out because you're headed for hell. Nothing makes for a greater recipe of co-dependency than being internally tag-teamed by that dynamic duo of insecurity and vulnerability. This is why it is important to channel the vulnerability into a passion outside of self. This is the only way to ward off insecurity, for insecurity cannot exist where there is an external focus. Vulnerability, however, is so powerful in its own right that, when properly channeled, it can do nothing but create, and greatness abounds.

A friend said to me recently, "A work of art is anything that a person creates that causes another person to think." She said that to say, there are many artists who do not create works of art. What is lacking in these artists is, yes you guessed it, vulnerability.

Many people are putting out works for the sole purpose of making money, the work sells, and they do well because it's distracting, and people do not want to have to think. They want to sit around blissfully enjoying mindless entertainment, and greedy people see the market and accommodate them, for a small fee.

These people call themselves artists because they either like the title, or recognize that they have an underutilized gift. They create what many may call art, but all will recognize the genius lacking in it. All will see that crazy does not live in them, and they will not be remembered long after they are gone because they did not make us think while they were here.

People who evoke emotion-based thought will linger longer in your memory than those who mindlessly entertain. They will appeal to the masses even when the masses resist, and even if it doesn't occur until years after the loss of their life, the masses will recognize the person, once deemed crazy, was a genius.

The scientists have it so easy. They write down what they are working on, do tests, and have support groups that help them by acting as sounding boards and challenging, or questioning, them for the possibility of errors. Any work they leave uncompleted, some other scientist can come, pick up, and continue where the first left off. In the end, they have the proof of their genius in the form of a formula, or a concoction that heals, or takes away the effects of some disease, or ailment.

Engineers also get to see the manifestation of their genius, in the planes we fly, the cars we drive, and all of the appliances, devices, and gadgets we have come to use and rely on daily. They have created the things that we never thought possible, and most of us dared not dream we could manifest.

For an artist though, it's different. The artist is only recognized if his words, lyrics, sketches, or paintings get through to, and/or impact, the right people. Hell, most of us would settle for being recognized by any one person, we don't even so much care if it is the "right people," and that is what puts artists in the most vulnerable position of all. For all of their attempts to hide and disguise their vulnerability, they put it out there in the open, on display to be peered at, and judged, by all the world; all of that, just because they can't find the damned words to tell the right people what they really feel inside.

Engineers and scientists channel their vulnerability, but they don't have to put it on display for the world until it has been tested, and proven, and they are sure that it works. Until then, they are only opening themselves up to the judgment of their peers who also clearly see their vision and the possibilities that lie within it. For someone like me, I count them fortunate that they are less susceptible to judgment, and criticism, but the truth is that my point of view is not at all their reality.

Their reality is much more bleak and lonely than I am painting it to be. The reality for them is that what lies in their head only has value if they can get it out and make it work, and if somebody else beats them to it, they are not recognized at all.

Imagine what it must feel like to go through life thoroughly and completely afraid to interact with the outside world for fear of the judgments they will make against you. Then one day, you find something you thoroughly enjoy and you work on it diligently, knowing in your heart that if the world sees your name attached to this work of genius, your life will be forever changed. People will no longer shun you, they will recognize you for the genius you are, and they will approach you with love and joy in their eyes instead of the disdain to which you have become accustomed.

Only, this fantasy at the helm of coming true is not realized due to the fact that the project is never completed, or worse yet, the project is completed and successful, and someone else takes credit for it. Could you imagine a worse fate? Yes, I could as well, but for those that suffer this fate it is as good as being invisible or dead.

We would like to believe that these visionaries and masterminds risk ego and sanity for the greater good and approval of humanity. The truth of the matter is these people have no choice. They have to get it out. They say whatever doesn't kill you makes you stronger, but the other truth is whatever you don't get out of you can kill you. We all love these people, but we have to love them from the distance they keep between us in order to remain in that creative state.

Where is it written, and why is it, that creativity has to come from a place of isolation? Not only that, but how is it we manage to isolate ourselves in the midst of so many people? It makes one appreciate the powers of the mind and of God that he could put it in our hearts and minds to find ways to manifest our abilities in spite of whatever may be going on around us, and in light of our own personal tragedies.

That we must suffer to create great works is our blessing as well as our curse. Our tragedy becomes our triumph. We live, we deal, we cope, we split, and then we create. We must truly be created in God's image, for only a God who creates man in his image can create men and women who create works that we all admire. What a loving God we have! Only the greatest of beings would be so thorough and heartfelt in creating us mere disposable mortals in His own image and providing us with the opportunity to be immortalized in the minds and hearts of the masses. I love you, YHWH!

Action Plan: For Finding Your Genius

1. Look deep inside yourself, until you find the thing that scares you. Now go do that.
2. Set aside time every day to work on your craft. No matter how much natural talent you have, success is still ultimately the product of work.
3. Put your heart and soul into your work, and tell your truth. The stuff of genius is **not** mass-produced. If you look, act, or sound, like somebody else, then you're not telling your truth.
4. If you need a break, take one. It's okay to stop, and explore other interests; it is not okay to quit because of fear of failure.
5. Be bold, and ignore the critics. They are only criticizing you because they are too afraid to explore their own truth.

Mirror Mirror

Stop! Do not waste one minute more complaining about another person; not your boss, coworker, spouse, nor anyone else you know. Instead, look in the mirror, and think about that person. Think about what it is that you don't like about them. What quality is it you see in them that drives you absolutely mad? As you think about the worst things about this person, look closely at your self because they are simply mirroring you.

You see, the lesson here is that everything you love, and everything you hate about a person, is your mind recognizing a quality in you that you either express or suppress. When you come in contact with people who have the qualities you express, you see them as kindred spirits, and invite them into your circle; they become your friends. Sadly, when you see a person with a quality you suppress, you feel an aversion to them. The tendency towards them is usually somewhere along the lines of contempt, disdain, and in some rare cases blatant persecution.

174

I know there will be a reluctance amongst most of the people reading this to accept it as a personal truth, so what I will do here now is show my own discovery of how I embody what I most despise, and how I made my peace with it, to the extent that I have thus far.

The two qualities I find most despicable are manipulation, and dishonesty, which can only mean, based on my above theory, that I am a manipulative liar. It is not a title I would generally give myself, nor one I am anxious to accept, but those close to me have called me this before, and I have such a strong aversion to these things that I have to find the truth in it.

So, here is what I know for sure. I am very capable of manipulating people; not just capable, I am good at it. For this reason I avoid people who are easily manipulated. It bothers me to think that I am taking unfair advantage of a person, so when I perceive that I am in the company of a person who I could potentially manipulate, I remove myself from their presence.

I keep company only with people who are capable of telling me no and meaning it. I often find my feelings getting hurt by such people because they usually do not take into consideration the fact that I too have feelings, which I suppose is fair because I denied them myself for many years.

With regard to manipulation, I had been using avoidance tactics to compensate for this tendency for so long, I had never even noticed I was doing it. When people started accusing me of being manipulative, I was greatly offended. I wondered how anyone could say that about me when I worked so hard to not be that. Then, I began to wonder if it was true, and if it was true, why did I not use it to my benefit? I still have no answer for that, but today I find myself asking the same question about lying.

I consider myself one of the most honest people I know. Granted I am aware that I can be deceitful, but I don't see deception as being the same as lying, at least that is how I justify it in my mind. However, I have people in my life who frequently accuse me of lying, and though I will admit there are rare occasions on which I have lied, I do not believe that they warrant me being called a liar. I mean today is March 3rd, and I can count on one hand the number of times that I have lied this year, and that includes acts of deception, but it does not include comedy. I put that in a whole other category.

The point is, I hate telling lies, and I hate being lied to, but no matter how strongly I confess, and protest these things, I am still brought face to face with the haunting truth that on some level, I am so greatly affected by it, because it is what I am.

My first reaction, upon realizing this truth, was of course denial, for what liar would admit to being such a thing? My second reaction was acceptance, for after all, I am only human. I can scarcely be expected to be perfect. My third reaction, justification, for there must be some excusable reason why I lied in the first place. My fourth reaction was guilt, which prompted me to ask for forgiveness for being such a horrible lying person. I am now somewhere between reactions five and six, which are acceptance with, and without, prejudice.

I find myself trying to understand why I judge lying so harshly, while at the same time wondering; if it is a quality that is a part of who I am, why not embody it more fully? Why not embrace it and profit from it? Why not use my gift to my advantage? I mean, that is why we are given these gifts, is it not? The downside is that these actions may negatively affect, or hurt others; but I wonder if I walk around with a disclaimer that I am a liar, so that people will know not to believe me, if that will help.

I do not inherently feel that a liar is what I want to be. It is neither how I see myself, nor how I wish to be seen. So what can I do about it? Nothing, I suspect. I cannot seem to make myself feel good about being that, and I cannot seem to stop. It's like so many things in my life. No matter what I do I am judged, not according to my actions, but according to my energy. Apparently, I have the energy of a manipulative, lying, flirtatious, stuck up bitch, but a lovable one.

After reaching this conclusion, I noticed a change in the way I interacted with others. I no longer judged them as harshly. By accepting that I possessed these qualities, I was able to see other people for whom they were, not what they did, and not how I perceived what they did affected me. I could see that their actions, like mine, were done not as a way to deliberately hurt me, as I had initially thought, but as a means of self protection from what they anticipated would be a negative consequence for their action.

Now, when I see people behave in such a way, I don't judge them harshly according to my own standards and beliefs. I look at them with love and compassion, knowing the road ahead of them is not an easy one.

For some of you, the issues are not going to be manipulation and lying. You may have a problem with someone who keeps up a lot of drama. If you look at yourself closely though, I am sure you will find that you too have a drama-filled life. You may feel like you have a lot of haters not realizing all of the hate you spew on others. It could be that you don't like cheaters but disregard or justify all of your little infidelities.

So I guess the point is this. Whatever your issues with others are, if you look for the same things in yourself and acknowledge it—you don't even have to fully understand it, just acknowledge it—doing so will make you a more loving, compassionate, and accepting person. As a result, all of your relationships will be enhanced.

Update: Since the original writing, I have progressed to the final level in this process, which is appreciation. I have now come to a place where I admire the creativity and skill it takes to be convincingly misleading. I see it as an art form like miming, or being a human statue, or pottery, or poetry. It is a talent, and a gift that when properly nurtured can make for wondrous entertainment. I still don't like being directly lied to, or manipulated, but in this regard, I have learned to let universal laws do what they were put in place to do. The one that applies here is that you can't con an honest man.

It is not the intentions of another, but our own, we must observe when evaluating whether or not someone is trying to mislead or manipulate us. If we are attempting to do something deceitful, we are likely in the company of like minds and therefore in danger of being deceived. That being the case, if we desire to protect ourselves from those who would bring us harm, we must purify our intentions.

Action Plan: For Seeing Yourself Clearly

1. Consider the things you dislike in people and write them down, and then try to find the ways in which you are those things.
2. Now work through the steps mentioned in the chapter until you get to a place of appreciation for what you once detested.
3. Enjoy the world and the people around you with your newfound perspective.

If You're Doing Something You Don't Enjoy, Stop!

Life is too short to spend being miserable. If you can in any moment of your life pinpoint a thought, action, location, or relationship that diminishes your quality of life, remove yourself from that situation at your earliest convenience. There is no reason to permit negativity to enter your realm knowingly.

In a conversation I recently had with my sister, she expressed concern about her husband calling to curse her out. I asked her why she would let someone call her to curse her out. She seemed confused by the question. "He is going to be mad," she said, "and when he gets mad he starts yelling and cursing at me. I can't control him."

"You may not be able to control his reaction," I told her, "but you can control how much of it you tolerate." I went onto explain to her that phones were created with this invaluable button that allows you to end any call you no longer want to continue. If someone calls you and begins assaulting your ears with words you find defamatory, or inappropriate, hang up the phone. If they call you back, and begin the same line of conversation, hang up again. In fact, do not engage in a conversation at all, unless the person you are talking to begins speaking in a way you find acceptable. This is how you teach people how to treat you; create a standard for yourself, and don't settle for anything other than that.

"Well what about when he comes home and starts yelling?" She asked.

I told her, "It's real simple; you leave. Explain to him very politely that you have no intention of allowing him to speak to you disrespectfully, and inform him that you are leaving to give him time to regain his composure and that you will return when he is capable of speaking to you civilly."

I heard the fear creep into her voice as she said, "Well what if he leaves me?"

I knew that was the real issue. That is always the real issue. The fear of being alone is so strong that it allows us to accept being mistreated and abused. "If he leaves you because you demand to be treated with respect, then he didn't want to be with you in the first place. He wanted a punching bag, not a relationship, and so long as you were willing to be that, he was going to stick around and keep throwing verbal punches. But it was only going to get worse, and you deserve better than that. Being alone is better than that."

I told her I had just gone through a similar transformation with my brother, and though he would be my brother for life, and could not actually leave me, the principles, and the outcome were still the same. At the point that this occurred, my brother and I lived together, which we had not done since we were both teenagers. Our relationship had, therefore, not progressed much beyond that of our youth.

As kids, we would fight, argue, yell, and cuss each other out, but as an adult I had experienced a side of life that made those things intolerable to me. Initially, when my brother would speak to me disrespectfully, I would respond in kind telling myself it was the only thing he understood. Then I realized I was feeding his behavior and lowering my energy to a level at which I did not wish to operate.

One day, I finally stopped. He called me in a rage, determined to let me know how he felt about one thing or another, and I just hung up the phone. He called back cursing, and I did it again. The next time he called, I answered the phone saying, "If you're not going to talk to me in a reasonable tone I will hang up again."

Believing himself to be amusing, he started off speaking civilly and then began raising his voice to get his point across. The minute his voice went up, I hung up the phone. I did not answer any more of his calls.

When he came home, he was mad. He tried to yell at me, and I told him, "If you start yelling, it will be at the wall because I am not going to be around to hear it. You either speak to me with respect or not at all."

He said to me very calmly, "That's okay because I am going to do the same thing to you. Watch next time you try to talk to me like that I am just going to hang up on you."

"Please do," I told him. "I would very much like it to be brought to my attention because that pattern of behavior has no place in my life. If I do it I am not aware of it, and I would very much like if you would give me the opportunity to recognize, and correct it."

He looked at me perplexed, said "whatever man," and walked away.

True to his word, the next time I yelled at him he hung up on me, and I smiled to myself immediately recognizing what I had done.

We both grew a lot that year, for you see it is only by means of awareness that you even recognize a problem exists, and you have to recognize it in order to change it. The same principle applies to every aspect of your life. If you find yourself spending time somewhere you don't want to be, recognize that you don't want to be there and leave. It is really very simple.

If you are doing something you don't enjoy, stop. No one is forcing you to be there. Evaluate what actions got you into that situation. Discover what you would rather be doing, and finally, ascertain a plan of action that will get you from where you are to where you want to be.

I had a job once that I absolutely detested. I was working at the front desk of a high-end hotel spa that catered only to very wealthy people. As the hotel had only recently opened, our client list was relatively small, and I was left with a lot of free time to sit behind the counter playing video games on the computer, trying to look busy.

My job description was to set appointments, check people in, and smile as I walked the guest back to the changing room or on a tour of the facility.

I felt like my brain cells were deteriorating from lack of use, and I was bored to tears, literally. So much so that I found myself one day actually calling in sad to work.

I dropped my kids off and started driving in the direction of my job, but somewhere along the way, tears began to descend from my eyes. The closer I got to my job the harder I was crying. I entered the freeway and had to get immediately back off, because at that point, I was bawling and could not see through the tears well enough to drive.

I sat there in my car uncertain of what to do, and the only option that seemed to offer relief was calling in. So I did. I called and told my supervisor that I could not go to work because I could not stop crying. She asked me if I wanted to come in and talk about, but I could not very well tell her it was the idea of coming in that was making me cry. I opted instead to just tell her no thank you; it was something I had to work out on my own.

When I hung up the phone, I felt immediate relief, until I got the notion that I would have to return the following day. I ended up in a park, walking around in circles barefoot for hours, just talking to my God, and myself, trying to figure out what I was going to do.

The only logical conclusion I could come up with was to quit. I use the word logical here loosely because on paper it made no sense. I had no other source of income and an insurmountable amount of debt, but at that point, none of that mattered.

Through my talks with God I felt assured I would be okay, and I stepped out on faith. It was a very difficult time during which I had to make a lot of compromises in my belief system, but when it was all said and done, I was fine. I was better than fine. I was back on track, and I had gotten exactly what I asked for.

So now, regarding your situation, I can say with certainty that change will not be easy. In fact it will be uncomfortable at best, but getting to the other side of it is pure bliss. In the moment when it feels the most difficult, or even like you are going backwards, keep in mind that you spent years creating the life you have, and the process of changing it takes time, patience, and determination. That is simply the price you pay for living your life enjoyably and on your terms.

Action Plan: For Receiving Proper Treatment

1. At any point in your life where you find yourself in a situation you don't prefer to be in, remove yourself.
2. If you find yourself being disrespected on the telephone, hang up.
3. If leaving your situation immediately does not seem like a viable option, create an action plan.

Focus on the Goal

Few things achieve faster results than resolute focus. Thoughts are things, and the longer and harder you focus your thoughts on whatsoever it is you desire the more likely you are to manifest it. If you have a goal that you want to see come to fruition, single-minded determination along with a lot of faith is the key. Keep in mind though that faith without works is dead.

Once you know what you want and you have wholehearted faith that you will and can have it, you have to start working toward getting it. This could take mental preparation or actual physical work. It can be manual labor, or psychological development, but either way, it is going to be something that is going to render you success.

The key to the work aspect of the process is to not stop working until you acquire whatever it is that you are working towards. There are going to be times when this is going to be very trying. At certain points it may even feel impossible, but do not give up. Giving up is like shouting from the rooftop, "I do not deserve this!" Just keep working and preparing, knowing that right there on the other side of that desire to give up is the success you've been longing to attain.

It is virtually a proven fact that every person who has attempted to be successful in any avenue of life has achieved that success only after they got passed the point where they wanted to give up. In many cases, this also happens right after they lose everything, or are on the verge of losing everything. When all hope looks lost, and there doesn't seem like there is a possible way out, a way appears, or an opportunity presents itself.

That is the way God operates. A miracle is only a miracle when there is no other way. However, if you're not even willing to work for what you supposedly want, why should anybody else work on it for you? If you're not doing the work, the consensus is that you really don't want it bad enough because if you did, you would be doing what it takes to get it. God, the universe, and even other people will go out of their way to help the person who is diligently trying to help himself by working toward his own goal.

As for the person who just sits around talking about what he wants, these sources will all be glad to just listen. In some cases, maybe even talk about his goals with him, but very few will lift a finger to help the person who is not lifting his own fingers.

This is partly because the law of investment states; "It is an unwise investment to invest in a person who will not invest in him or her self." Work is a form of investment. It is an investment of time and energy.

Generally, the more you value and believe in your objective the harder you will work because there is a satisfaction that comes from one, doing the work, and two, seeing the work complete. That sense of accomplishment that comes from a job well-done often makes the work worth it even in the absence of the miracle, and that is how you can tell that the miracle is coming. When you can look at the work that you are doing or have done and say that it is good, then on some level, it enhances your faith, and your knowledge that the thing you want most is on its way.

This is even more fulfilling when the thing you most want is the thing you are working on, and the completion of it alone is its own validation. When you can look at the work of your own hands and know that the miracle was in your ability to overcome obstacles, such as lack of ability or resources, and know that your blood, sweat, and tears went into this project, and here it is before you, and it is good, that is a wonderful feeling. Satisfaction comes not so much in the process as in the completion and in the character and appreciation it builds in you along the way.

While you sit back admiring your completed or nearly completed project, wondering what is going to happen with it, I want you to keep in mind that no one does it alone. You have done the hard part. You did the work. You focused on the goal until it was completed, or you got to a place where there was nothing more you could do. Now, you ask for help.

Nobody achieves success in this world without the help of others. You may have to pay them for their help, but that doesn't make it any less other people's help that gets you to your goal.

It's like I told my very proud teenage son one day when he was struggling with his homework. Actually, he wasn't just struggling with his work; he was failing his class. I asked him what the problem was, and he told me he didn't understand how to do the work. So I asked him why he didn't just ask me to help him. His reply was something to the effect that he did not like asking for help. I told him if that were true he was in for a very hard life.

I told him that in this world there are two types of people. There are those who ask for help, and those who are asked to help. You can be both types, but if you are not at least the one asking, your success will be limited. You see, the people at the top of any field are the people that asked the greatest number of people for help. They don't ever stop asking. They have a goal, they are focused, and they will do whatever they have to do and ask whoever they believe can help them until the goal is accomplished.

The people who don't ask for help sit around wishing, hoping, and praying for a break. Even when offered help, they sometimes turn it down out of pride or some false sense of hubris. They have been misled into believing that there is some vanity in going it alone, in pulling yourself up by your bootstraps and making it on your own. Know now that anyone who tells you that they achieved success without the assistance of someone else is lying. It isn't possible. The world is designed in such a way that we are all connected. None among us can make it without the aid of at least one other person.

Evidence of this can be seen in the neo-natal ward of the hospital. Studies have shown that babies who don't receive attention or affection from another living being are less likely to survive. This phenomenon, of an untouched life ending too soon, does not decline as we get older. The pain of feeling alone in this world is what leads people to commit suicide. The point is; we all need each other. So whether you're asking a few people for just enough to survive, or you're asking a lot of people for enough to thrive, grow, and build, you are still asking.

Don't be a master of minimalism. If you have a worthy aspiration, don't stop working and asking for help until you achieve it. Stay focused on the goal, and you may surprise yourself. It may just turn out to be bigger and better than you ever thought possible.

Now, while I advise you to seek help, I implore you to not attempt to manipulate others in the process. There are people who have a genuine desire to give you what you need. Your objective is to find them. Do not try to use, mistreat, underpay, or manipulate anyone into helping you, or you will sabotage yourself.

For it is written: "Now, however, there remain faith, hope, love, these three; but the greatest of these is love." That quote is taken from the Bible at 1Corinthians 13:13. It helps us to appreciate the importance of love. I personally find it ironic that love is mentioned all throughout the Bible as being the greatest most important thing we can do, have, or be, and yet we spend the vast majority of our time with our energy otherwise engaged and wonder why we are so unhappy.

We tend to think that by being out for self, we are showing love for ourselves, but nothing could be further from the truth. The truth is that the greatest demonstration of self-love is the love you show toward the people with whom you come in contact and the energy you put into the work that you do.

It's kind of funny the way that works, and I am only speaking on this because I, too, was deceived into believing that if I invested my energy into getting everything I could out of other people I was somehow doing myself a favor. I could not have been more wrong. It was at a point in my life where I became overwhelmed by an urge to give that I began to understand the real truth.

I learned that by giving time energy and love, I was able to multiply these things in my own life. The same holds true for money, but we will talk about that later. With love, the more you put out, the more you get back. Accordingly, the more energy you put into that which you love, the more energy you acquire to continue to invest in that application. Love begets love, and energy begets energy, but where time is concerned, you may be inclined to disagree with me. Just hear me out.

I am not implying that by giving your time you will add a single moment to your life because that is not my place to say. Only God can determine the span of a person's life. With regard to time, what you will gain is value. The quality of your life can be enhanced by the time you give, and the value of your time will be multiplied.

With regard to your desires though, the love you give to the things you want multiplies the speed with which you attain them. So much so that what at one point may have seemed unattainable suddenly seems to happen overnight.

This is where the connection between love, time, and energy comes in. When you fully love the things you desire, time seems to fly by while you are engaged in activities concerning them. You, therefore, end up giving it more time than you had intended to, and the joy you feel in the process increases your energy level giving you more joy, love, and energy to continue to devote.

Before you know it, you have invested hours that flew by and energy you didn't know you had into this one thing and often for nothing more than love.

More importantly though, the manifestation of a creation, or product conceived in love will touch others in such a way that they will pay whatever you ask, or whatever value you assign to this thing borne of your love. That is why it is often said do what you love, and the money will come. I have once heard it phrased better, that if you do what you love, the pleasure of knowing you've done what you loved will come.

That is why I did not include money in this formula, because the reality is that money has its own rules. Although money does follow the basic rule of thumb that the more you give the more you will receive, the other rules that govern money are designed not just to help you receive it, but to ensure that you hold onto it.

If you can't do what you love, change your vocabulary until words like can't no longer have a place in it. If you don't know what you love, then love what you do, and eventually it will work out so that what you love, and what you do are the same thing. To the degree that this becomes true for you is the degree to which you will be able to measure your successes in life by the quality of your time, the level of your energy, and the abundance of your love. When this is your reality, the money too will be there, but it will no longer matter.

Action Plan: For Achieving Your Goals

1. If you have a goal, focus your full attention on it, and work towards it until you achieve it.
2. If you don't know your goal, give your whole heart in service to whatever you are presently doing, as it is assuredly a stepping-stone to your purpose.
3. Use your time wisely; do not squander it. It's the one thing once spent you cannot get back.
4. Use affirmations to increase the amount of energy and love you put out. Instead of saying I'm tired (which is depleting), say I am bursting with energy.

The Three words we should not use
And the two we should (I am)

In 2007, I realized that I wanted to be a public speaker. I kept saying to myself, "I want to be a public speaker." I read books on how to become a public speaker, and their advice basically amounted to, write a book. I read books on how to write, and market a book, and I gathered from them that, to properly market a book, I needed a public speaking platform. I felt like I was applying for credit, or my first job, all over again.

It was the cycle of life, as I had known it. To get credit you had to have credit, and to get a job, you had to have had a job. It was extremely difficult to get someone to take a chance on me without providing evidence that I was worth taking a chance on. Ergo, the only way to provide such evidence was to show that someone else had already taken a chance on me.

Ironically, it did not matter what the outcome of that initial arrangement was; all that mattered was that it existed. I knew people who had gotten jobs, and then within weeks got fired from their job and still had an easier time getting hired than someone who never had a job in the first place. It seemed that the mere fact that they had a first job was the only prerequisite to getting another job.

That is the way credit works as well. We have all heard the saying that bad credit is better than no credit. Well it's true; no matter how bad you mess up your credit, it is still deemed by creditors as being better then not having any at all. I think these things are so because of the desire of people to want to believe that we learn from our mistakes.

The point is, I was back to the beginning of what appeared to be a repeating pattern. I was once again faced with the same predicament and no idea how to overcome it. What I failed to realize at the time was that the problem with my approach to getting what I wanted was not what I perceived to be the cycle of life but my mindset regarding life.

I had spent a great deal of my life getting exactly what I wanted and could not understand why, when it came to this, I was having so much trouble, even though it was something I wanted desperately. It took me years, and a mind more brilliant than my own, to help me understand that it was the want itself keeping me from having my hearts desire, but I will explain that more later.

Fast-forward to the year 2008. I was invited by a friend to attend a live comedy performance featuring Mo'Nique and Steve Harvey at the Phillips arena. I sat there in the nosebleed section of the stadium in complete awe of this very brazen and robust woman who spoke with so much authority and confidence. She was loud and proud in vocalizing her issues, her problems, and the pain from her past with a vulnerability that heightened incessantly until the only way to diffuse the mounting negativity permeating the building was to laugh.

She stood up there and expressed herself from the heart with so much emotion, and passion, and as she did so, she would chuckle as if to keep from crying, and we would laugh right along with her. We would clap for her successes in overcoming her obstacles and getting back at her villains, and we would roar, hoot, and howl at the experience itself. It was cathartic; the release of emotional energy that erupted out of us in what is commonly referred to as the best medicine.

I watched the audience's reaction with amazement and all I could think to myself is, Christy you can do that. It could be you up there in front of all of these people telling your stories and diffusing them with humor so that the audience can laugh with you at your pain. That could be you one day getting paid significant sums of money for selling out Phillips arena. In that moment, I believed so strongly that I could make a real difference by being on stage that I decided I would start performing stand-up comedy.

On my way home that night I picked up a paper that detailed the popular events going on around the city and immediately began searching for a place to perform. Two days later I went to Apache, a culturally rich, rustic bar on the outskirts of downtown Atlanta, and I performed a piece of poetry I had written years before. I guess it was my way of getting my feet wet or working up my nerve, because I had never even done that before.

The following day I went to Kat's Café, a chic little lounge in the heart of downtown Atlanta, and I performed my first bit of stand-up. I had researched the different places around town that offered open mic comedy on various nights of the week, and I found that the first available possibility would be on a Monday. There were two locations that reported having a comedy night but only one of them said it was an open mic.

I went to the open mic first. When I arrived I inquired about the procedure for signing up to perform and was introduced to the host Rot-knee. I told him I had an interest in performing, and he told me his list was full, but I was welcome to stay, and watch, or even call to reserve a spot on the next show. I thanked him for the information, and headed off to the next place.

When I made it to the next location, which was Kat's, I asked the waitress where I could find the person in charge of the show. I was then introduced to Maurice and told that he was the promoter and as such the person I would need to talk to about getting on the lineup. I introduced myself and told him I was a new comedian looking for an open mic for my first performance. He told me that they were not doing open mic;

they were just doing a showcase and that I could not perform, but I was welcome to watch.

He proceeded to introduce me to all of the other comedians that were there. Then he introduced me to Karlous who was the host of the comedy show. Upon meeting me, Karlous offered me the opportunity to perform, against Maurice's wishes. I told him that I would love to in so many words. I think my exact reaction was the shaking of my head "No," as my mouth said "Uh sure."

"Ok." he said, "I will let you do some time."

I was terrified. In fact, it was the single most terrifying experience of my entire life, and I loved every minute of it. I had no idea what I was going to say. In retrospect, I don't even know what I said, but I did make a few people laugh, and that is how my comedy career was born.

I hold a lot of beliefs about that night and the way things happened. I believe that Karlous and Maurice actually argued for a good ten minutes about whether or not I could perform, and Karlous ultimately won. I also believe that had he not given me the chance on that night I may never have tried again. I even believe that I was there not of my own accord but because of the direction of a power greater than me. After all, I had wanted to be a public speaker, not a comedienne.

This brings me back to what I have learned about wants and the difference between the public speaking career I wanted and the comedy career I got. The more I wanted to write a book or become a speaker, the more want I created in myself. What I am saying is, as I read it so eloquently put in a book by Neal Donald Walsh, You can't have what you want, because the thought "I want" just creates a greater experience of wanting.

In order to have the experience of having, it is necessary to make a more declarative statement, such as I am going to write, or speak, or whatever it is you intend to do. I did not want to do comedy, I declared; "I am going to do comedy."

I believed not only that I was capable, but also that I would be doing the world a disservice by not pursuing it, and the next thing I knew, I was doing it. The most fascinating thing to me is that for four years while I did comedy, and continued to want to do public speaking, it didn't occur to me that it was my own want that was preventing me.

So often we use these limiting words in our speech and do not realize the impact they have on our lives. The word *can't* is a self fulfilling prophecy. You render yourself capable by declaring that you are, and by stating that you are not, you create that reality as well. This truth is commonly accepted but rarely adhered to.

Another limiting word I discovered was holding me back was the word *try*. I was in a business meeting one day and I told the man I was meeting with that I would try to have a presentation to him by a deadline of my choosing. In response, he said to me, "Try to hit yourself."

The statement initially disturbed me. I found it rude, and a bit insulting, but he persisted. It was then that I saw the point he was making. It was only after I realized the meaning of his words that he explained it to me. He said, "no matter how hard you try you cannot hit yourself. You either do, or you don't. The same is true for everything in life."

I wanted to disagree with him. I wanted to cite examples from my own personal life where I had been trying to write a book for years, and a whole slew of other things I was trying to do, or had tried to do. The fact was that all the things I had tried to do were things that were still undone.

Unfortunately, or perhaps fortunately, the truth is undeniable, and I have been blessed to recognize it when I hear it, so I conceded. He was right. You can't try to do anything. You either do it, or you don't.

I then told him definitively that I would have the project to him by the deadline, and I knew that because I had resolved to get it done. I was going to make it happen; one way or another. I felt in that moment an immediate shift in my perspective; much like the one I felt when I understood the purpose that wanting serves.

It occurred to me that all of these words served as tactics I had employed to buy myself time, avoid making a decision, or give myself an out when I didn't get through with what I had set out to do. I further realized that the only thing I was stalling with these tactics was my own progress. It was then that I chose to remove them from my daily vocabulary.

The result as you see is that I have written the book, and I am speaking publicly. What I will say though, regarding this whole experience, is that there was no better training ground for public speaking than stand-up comedy. I recognized it from the moment I started, and I feel even more strongly about it today.

So what I want to encourage you to do now is remove the words want, can't, and try from your vocabulary, and replace them with the two most powerful words in existence; I am. They are two of the smallest words, but they have a veritable impact. The minute you put those two words together in a sentence, you begin shaping your future.

Other declarative statements work as well. You can say I will, I can, I have, and so forth, and by doing so, you ordain the statements that follow to be true, but by saying I am, you declare not only your intentions to do something, but who and what you are as a being. More than a statement, it is a proclamation, and the more you use it the more useful you will find it.

Action Plan: For Positive Speaking

1. Monitor your daily declarations, notice how often you use words like want, try, or can't, and observe the outcome regarding these things.
2. Spend one day where you don't use those words at all. Replace them with I will, I am, or I can, and notice the difference in what you accomplish.
3. If you don't notice a difference then it is possible that your subconscious doesn't believe you. Fret not, you can convince it over time with the use of affirmations.
4. Look for other negative words you can eliminate from your vocabulary and other positive words you can replace them with.

Live Your Story

We all have life, but we do not all truly live. I want to encourage you to live like you were dying. Every morning when you wake, ask yourself; if today were my last day on earth what would I do with it? For some people, finding answers to this question will be rather difficult. I know that this is a tumultuous time for many people, whose lives are filled with so much turmoil; it's hard to navigate through it all. So I have an aid that may help you.

Imagine yourself, as an elderly person at the end of your years. Your grandchildren and even great-grandchildren come to visit you a little more regularly, because their parents keep telling them you won't be alive much longer. When they come, they ask you all about your life. Now think about the story you would like to be able to tell them. Say it to yourself now as if you were telling it to them then. Take note of as many details as you can. Write them down if possible as a reference.

Now, go live that life. Find a way to make all of those stories you just told your grandchildren true. If you are contemplating divorce, but in your story you were with your same husband your entire life, find a way to work it out and stay together. If you did something that changed the world, start doing it. The end of your life may seem a long way off, but the story of how you lived it is taking place right now, so live your story. Embrace every moment of it, and take note, because often the most painful and trying times make for the best part of your story.

I will share with you an example of a small part of my story where I was fully alive and aware of everything going on around me. This is just to illustrate some of the ways in which you can embrace life and enhance your experience of living.

I had packed up my children and moved to the Caribbean to help my mother with her business. I had lived there as a child but hadn't been back in years. My mother was stressed out and in need of assistance, and I thought it would be a good experience for my children. When I arrived, I was reminded of how much this place had meant to me and how different it was from home.

This Island was alive with stimuli for the senses. The smells that filled the air were pure and untainted. There was the smell of salt in the breeze coming off of the ocean, but more fragrant than that was the food being cooked right on the street. Everywhere you turned offered the opportunity for an assault on the olfactory organs. Gasoline, exhaust, human body odor from people who seemed unaware of the purpose deodorant served.

There were more pleasant scents as well, like fresh baked bread, and fruit ripening on the tree. Oh, wasn't that a sight to behold; to see actual fruit on a tree. I don't know when last I saw that in an American city. This was certainly no American city. This place was full of vibrant colors that even Crayola could not do justice.

The people appeared poor, though not impoverished, but the land on this island was rich. It was vibrant and teeming with life. The ocean was full of that fish you could just look down and see swimming around you. On land, the dogs did not even seem threatened by moving vehicles. Everything here seemed to go at its own pace, and whoa to the person that tried to speed it up. At best, that would be an exercise in frustration.

The sounds included people yelling words I could not very well make out, and music, loud pulsing music, that seemed to come from every direction and pumped through my body as if my heart were beating to its rhythm. At night when I sat out on the balcony, the ocean itself seemed to carry the music from across the island directly to my doorstep. There were nights when I wished it didn't.

One night, in particular, I had a hard time with the sound of music pouring in over the ledge. It was so distressing it nearly made me want to throw myself over. It was not the music in general that affected me so. It was the particular song that was playing. Though I could not hear the words, I recognized the rhythm immediately, and it sent a pain through my stomach so sharp it was like I was being stabbed repeatedly with a serrated blade. I was doubled over by the unrelenting ache coursing through my mid-section, but I was fresh out of tears, which made it that much more unbearable.

I went inside to escape the melodic source of my melancholy only to discover that though my refuge blocked the sound from my ears. The effects of the music still lived on in my body. Like blood, it was flowing through me just under the skin, and my desire to escape it was matched in intensity by a desire to submerge myself in it. I wanted to breathe in the music, and hold onto it, because it was all I had left of him.

I was wrought with agony at this internal conflict, taking place inside of me, where reason was being cast aside, and emotion was tearing me down and turning me into a person my sane self could not recognize.

"Is that what love does?" I asked myself knowing full well there could only be one answer. All these years, I had thought myself to be in love, with more than one person and for varying periods of time, but never had I ever felt the thralls of distress, and despair, contrasted by the utter joy, and elation that I was enveloped in this time. If this was love, it was a love I never knew existed, and facing the prospect of having to live without it almost made me wish I could return to the blissfulness of ignorance.

However, the artist in me would not allow that. She knew that this was an experience that would change my range and elevate my art to the next level, and she insisted that I lived fully in each moment of it and experience all that it had to offer. There was no numbing, or blocking out the pain. I had to feel this. I had to fully know and encompass it. I had to consume it and make it a part of me. Only then, could I release it and put it back out.

The benefit here was that I did not go numb and shut off my feelings as I had in the past. This time I opened myself up to them, and allowed myself to be honest, and vulnerable about what I felt.

This created a space that was later able to be filled by the very person causing the pain; and the happiness I felt when he came back to me was much better than the bliss of ignorance.

I was there less than a year, and in that time, I managed to break hearts, have my own heart broken, mended, and crushed when I had to leave. It was the best, worst time of my life, and given the chance to do it all over again, I would without a doubt. It was like time sped up in this place, and a whole lifetime could be lived in a matter of months, but that is just one part of my story.

It is the part that taught me that recognizing what is happening in your life, in the moments that it happens, is powerful. It is a gift that should be developed because it gives you greater control over your story.

Action Plan: For living your life

1. Look at your situation objectively. Understand that you created it. Acknowledge it for what it is, and if it doesn't suit you, change it. Most likely, it is just there to warn you anyway.
2. I prefer to perceive negative situations as a wake up call, like a life alarm sounding to let you know you are drifting off course. When you correct your course you shift the direction of your life back to what you envisioned for yourself. The sooner you heed the warnings the less painful the experience.
3. Make your goal to become so adept at recognizing when you're getting away from your life story or purpose that you make the necessary changes immediately, and live a relatively pain free life as a result.
4. Write down what you want your story to be, and then compare it to what is going on in your life at any given moment. If what is going on doesn't match your story, you are off track. Knowing this give you the power to change it.